SECRETS AND LIES

Secrets and Lies

MIKE LEIGH

faber and faber
LONDON · BOSTON

First published in 1997
by Faber and Faber Limited
3 Queen Square London WC1N 3AU

Photoset by Parker Typesetting Service, Leicester
Printed in England by Clays Ltd, St Ives plc

Mike Leigh is hereby identified as author of this work in accordance with
Section 77 of the Copyright, Designs and Patents Act 1988

A CIP record for this book
is available from the British Library
ISBN 0-571-19291-2

2 4 6 8 10 9 7 5 3 1

SECRETS AND LIES

Secrets and Lies was first shown on 10 May 1996 at the Cannes Film Festival, where it was awarded the Palme d'Or. The cast and crew were as follows:

CYNTHIA	Brenda Blethyn
MAURICE	Timothy Spall
MONICA	Phyllis Logan
ROXANNE	Claire Rushbrook
HORTENSE	Marianne Jean-Baptiste
JANE	Elizabeth Berrington
PAUL	Lee Ross
DIONNE	Michele Austin
SOCIAL WORKER (JENNY)	Lesley Manville
STUART	Ron Cook
WOMAN WITH SCAR	Emma Amos
HORTENSE'S BROTHERS	Brian Bovell
	Trevor Laird
HORTENSE'S SISTER-IN-LAW	Claire Perkins
HORTENSE'S NEPHEW	Elias Perkins McCook
SENIOR OPTOMETRIST	June Mitchell
JUNIOR OPTICIAN	Janice Acquah
LITTLE GIRL IN OPTICIAN'S	Keeley Flanders
FIRST BRIDE	Hannah Davis
FIRST BRIDE'S FATHER	Terence Harvey
SECOND BRIDE	Kate O'Malley
GROOM	Joe Tucker
VICAR	Richard Syms
BEST MAN	Grant Masters
MOTHER IN FAMILY GROUP	Annie Hayes
FATHER IN FAMILY GROUP	Peter Wight
GRANDMOTHER	Jean Ainslie
TEENAGE SON	Daniel Smith
BOXER	Gary McDonald
NURSE	Lucy Sheen
YOUNG MOTHER	Frances Ruffelle
BABY	Felix Manley
DOG-OWNER	Alison Steadman
CAT-OWNER	Liz Smith
POTENTIAL HUSBAND	Nitin Chandra Ganatra

CONJUROR	Metin Marlow
RAUNCHY WOMEN	Amanda Crossley
	Su Elliott
	Di Sherlock
TRIPLETS	Alex Squires
	Lauren Squires
	Sade Squires
TRIPLETS' MOTHER	Sheila Kelley
LITTLE BOY	Dominic Curran
LITTLE BOY'S MOTHER	Angela Curran
MEN IN SUITS	Stephen Churchett
	Philip Davis
	David Neilson
	Peter Stockbridge
	Peter Waddington
GRADUATE	Rachel Lewis
GLUM WIFE	Wendy Nottingham
GRINNING HUSBAND	Paul Trussell
UNEASY COUPLE	Anthony O'Donnell
	Denise Orita
ELDERLY LADY	Margery Withers
LAUGHING COUPLE	Ruth Sheen
	Gordon Winter
ENGAGED COUPLE	Jonathan Coyne
	Mia Soteriou

Written and Directed by	Mike Leigh
Produced by	Simon Channing-Williams
Cinematographer	Dick Pope
Editor	Jon Gregory
Production Designer	Alison Chitty
Art Director	Eve Stewart
Costume Designer	Maria Price
Make-up	Christine Blundell
Music	Andrew Dickson
Sound Recordist	George Richards

A CiBy 2000/Thin Man production in association with
Channel Four Films

Daylight. A cemetery. A funeral cortège moves slowly under the trees past a cluster of Victorian gravestones.

Now the camera tracks through another part of the cemetery. In the distance we heard the singing of a hymn ('How Great Thou Art'). Gradually, the funeral is revealed. The singing gets louder. The funeral is well attended. Several men are filling in the grave. In the distance, beyond the trees, are two large gasometers.

We cut to a series of tighter shots, some groups and some close-ups, of mourners, who vary in age and sex. There are a few white people, but the vast majority are black: it is very much a West Indian funeral. They continue to sing the hymn.

We stay on one young woman for much longer than anybody else. She is maintaining her composure, but tears stream down her cheeks.

A wreath, forming the word 'MUM', is placed on the grave.

A large mansion with a neoclassical porch. A vintage two-tone Rolls Royce with white tyres and in wedding livery sits in the drive. The chauffeur stands by.

Inside, in a large drawing-room, a man in a formal suit – the PHOTOGRAPHER *– is arranging the bride's train on the floor. She is posed on a sofa, holding her bouquet.*

PHOTOGRAPHER: Let's make the most of this beautiful train . . .
   that's it – okay . . .
   (*He smiles at her, a friendly smile. He has a beard. He goes over to another sofa, and picks up a camera. A severe middle-aged man in a morning suit, presumably the bride's father, paces up and down in the doorway, occasionally looking at his watch. The* PHOTOGRAPHER *looks through his viewfinder.*)
   Yeah . . . that's really great, yeah – yeah. Okay, now, as I said before, you're under no obligation to, but you can if you want to give me a . . . tiny little twinkle – yeah, that is – (*He snaps.*) lovely! Get a bit closer . . .
   (*He does so. The bride looks nervous.*)
   Don't you worry – you'll be all right! (*He chuckles. He looks up from his camera, and adjusts a lock of her hair delicately.*)

I

There's just a little bit . . . that's it! And you've got an
eyelash on your nose – we don't want that, now we . . . (*He
removes it.*) Supposed to be on your eye, not on your
snitch.
(*He laughs, and the bride smiles.*)
That's it – you've got a lovely smile when you smile,
'aven't you? Right, okay; and keep that lovely gorgeous
smile! (*He snaps.*) That's lovely! I think that'll do for the
time being. Well done, Sarah! That's the easy bit.
(*He laughs. Sarah smiles, but her smile quickly fades.*)

In another house, in a room with a blue wall, a WOMAN *wearing
blue striped dungaree shorts stands stencilling leaves on to a blue Art
Nouveau umbrella stand. She works intensively.*

*Later, three children, one with a bicycle, run past a modern detached
house, shouting.*
    It is the stencilling WOMAN*'s house, and she is watching them
from her bay window. She is now wearing a fashionable matching
pair of grey trousers and a grey waistcoat. She turns to the*
PHOTOGRAPHER *from the previous scene. He is sitting in an
armchair, wearing an open-neck shirt and slacks.*
WOMAN: They make a noise, don't they?

PHOTOGRAPHER: At least they can play out round here.
WOMAN: I suppose so.
 (*She crosses to the mantelpiece. She is* MONICA. *The*
 PHOTOGRAPHER *is her husband,* MAURICE. *At the*
 mantelpiece, MONICA *adjusts a vase.* MAURICE *touches her*
 waistcoat.)
MONICA: What is it?
MAURICE: Is that a suit?
MONICA: It came as a combination.
MAURICE: Do they go together?
MONICA: Well, if you think they do, they do, and if you think
 they don't, they don't.
MAURICE: 'T's nice.
 (MONICA *turns to a framed photograph of a smiling little girl.*
 She adjusts its position.)
 Twenty-one in August.
MONICA: She is.
MAURICE: I used to worry meself sick when she played out.
MONICA: She survived it, though, didn't she?
 (*She sits on the sofa.*)
MAURICE: All things considering.
MONICA: She's back on the streets now.
MAURICE: I beg your pardon?!

3

MONICA: Well, she is, isn't she?

MAURICE: I don't 'arf miss 'er!

MONICA: I know . . . How long is it since we've seen her?

MAURICE: Two and a half years.

(MONICA *sighs*.)

MONICA: We could always ask her over.

MAURICE: I'd like to.

MONICA: For her birthday. It's only a couple of months away.

(MAURICE *chuckles*.)

What now?

MAURICE: 'Hey, Roxanne! What're you doing for your twenty-first?' 'I'm going over to my auntie and uncle's 'ouse for my birthday treat!!' (*He chuckles*.)

MONICA: It was only a suggestion.

MAURICE: She's probably doing her own thing.

MONICA: I suppose we'd have to invite . . . Cynthia, as well. There's no show without Punch.

MAURICE: I'm sure she'd like to see the place.

MONICA: Oh, I'm sure she would!

MAURICE: She can't help it.

MONICA: Can't she?

(*Pause.* MAURICE *gets up*.)

MAURICE: It's about time you showed if off; I mean, you've done a lovely job. (*He tops up their wine glasses – they are drinking red wine*.)

MONICA: I think so. (*She picks up a magazine*.)

MAURICE: I really must get down to see her.

MONICA: You speak to her on the phone, don't you?

MAURICE: It's not the same thing, though, is it?

MONICA: She's *your* sister.

MAURICE: I'm really proud of that portrait.

(MONICA *looks up at it. We see it in close-up*. ROXANNE *is grinning cheekily*.)

I reckon that's the last time she ever smiled.

A drab urban street. A young woman sweeps the pavement as people pass by. She puts the refuse into her handcart. She wears trousers and boots and a luminous safety-tunic. She looks glum. She is ROXANNE.

4

*In a bleak box factory, a sad-looking middle-aged woman stands
alone, operating a machine that cuts slits in sheets of cardboard. This
is* CYNTHIA.

CYNTHIA's *and* ROXANNE's *cramped, cluttered living-room.*
CYNTHIA *sits in an armchair, with a whisky,* ROXANNE *on the
sofa, smoking a cigarette. A tennis match can be heard on the
television.*

CYNTHIA: I don't know what's got into you lately.

ROXANNE: You complainin'?

CYNTHIA: No.

ROXANNE: Well shut up then.

CYNTHIA: Sit 'ere on me own for years on end . . . can't get you
to stop in at all, and now you never go out!

ROXANNE: Leave it out.

CYNTHIA: You've been sitting there for a month with a face like
a slapped arse.

ROXANNE: Well, what's there to smile about?
(*Pause.*)

CYNTHIA: Thought 'e might've phoned at the weekend. (*She
sips some whisky.*)

ROXANNE: 'Oo?

CYNTHIA: 'Oo d'you think? Ain't 'eard from 'im for ages.

ROXANNE: 'E's busy, ain' 'e?

CYNTHIA: We're all busy.

ROXANNE: 'E's got 'is weddin's an' that – it's the summer.

CYNTHIA: Out o' sight, out o' mind . . .

ROXANNE: Well, if you're that bothered, why don't you ring 'im
yourself? 'E's *your* brother!

CYNTHIA: I'm not runnin' up me phone bill! 'E knows where I
am if 'e wants me. 'E'd 'ave 'ad us up there to see it by
now, I expect, if it wasn't for 'er. Toffee-nosed cow . . .
What's 'e want with six bedrooms, anyway?
(*Pause.* ROXANNE *stubs out her cigarette.* CYNTHIA *takes
another swig of whisky. She is beginning to get a little drunk.*)
What's all your mates doin' tonight, then?

ROXANNE: I don't know – I ain't asked 'em.

CYNTHIA: You wanna get yourself a bloke. That's what you
wanna do!

5

ROXANNE: I've told you, I don't wanna get anything – I'm quite 'appy 'ere, thank you very much!

CYNTHIA: When I was your age, I could've 'ad the pick of the crop.

ROXANNE: Well, why didn't yer?

CYNTHIA: Because I lost my poor mother, that's why.

ROXANNE: Oh, 'ere we go!

CYNTHIA: I was stuck at 'ome from the age o' ten, lookin' after Maurice and yer grandad.

ROXANNE: Yeah, we know!

CYNTHIA: Then I got saddled with you! That was my downfall, darlin'!

ROXANNE: I didn't ask to be born!

CYNTHIA: No, an' I never asked to 'ave yer, neither!

ROXANNE: Well, you should've thought about that before you dropped yer knickers!

(ROXANNE *glares at the tennis, and* CYNTHIA *glares at* ROXANNE.)

A little GIRL *is having her eyes tested by an* OPTOMETRIST. *The* GIRL *is wearing an elaborate ophthalmological contraption on her eyes. The* OPTOMETRIST *holds a lens in front of the girl's right eye for a moment.*

OPTOMETRIST: With? Or without?

GIRL: I think without.

OPTOMETRIST: Without?

GIRL: Yeah.

OPTOMETRIST: Okay.

(*The* OPTOMETRIST *is the young woman who was crying at the funeral. Now she is friendly and cheerful. She is* HORTENSE.)

HORTENSE: What about this one? Better with . . . or without?

GIRL: I think this time it's with.

HORTENSE: With?

GIRL: Yeah.

HORTENSE: All right, we'll pop this one in, then. (*She does so.*) I hear you're a really good runner.

GIRL: Yeah – cross-country.

HORTENSE: Have you won anything?

6

GIRL: Not yet – I've only just started.

HORTENSE: Okay, then. Look up again. Now . . . this is going to blur a bit, but just tell me what you can read, okay?

GIRL: Yeah. (*She reads*) Haitch. L.A.C.T. . . .

HORTENSE: Right . . .

GIRL: An' I can't read any more.

HORTENSE: Okay, that's good! Very good – I'm gonna do your other eye now. (*She proceeds to do so.*)

HORTENSE *places the dust-cover over a large piece of eye-testing equipment. Moments later, she emerges from this back room into a bright, modern optometrist's shop. Another young woman, a junior* OPTICIAN, *sits behind the reception desk.*

OPTICIAN: You off, then?

HORTENSE: Yeah.

OPTICIAN: Got any plans for the weekend?

HORTENSE: Well, I've got to go to my mum's house, and sort through her things.

OPTICIAN: Oh, have you?

HORTENSE: Yeah.

OPTICIAN: Hope it goes all right.

HORTENSE: Well, it's gotta be done.

OPTICIAN: Yeah.

HORTENSE: Okay, then. (*She goes.*)

OPTICIAN: Right, I'll see you on Monday.

HORTENSE: Yeah. Have a nice weekend.

OPTICIAN: Cheers.

    (HORTENSE *turns back in the shop doorway.*)

HORTENSE: Ooh . . . Enjoy the christening!

OPTICIAN: I'll try.

HORTENSE: (*Laughing*) Okay, 'bye!

OPTICIAN: 'Bye!

    (HORTENSE *sets off down the busy street.*)

In her late mother's bedroom, HORTENSE *sits on the big bed. She is sifting through an old box of assorted letters, photographs, documents, passports, etc. She takes a note out of an envelope, glances at it, and puts it back. She picks up a string of beads. Gradually, heated voices begin to be heard downstairs.* HORTENSE *stops to listen.*

WOMAN: (*Downstairs*) It's ten past. We've got to pick Shalatika up.

MAN: (*Downstairs*) What're you talking about?

WOMAN: (*Downstairs*) We've got ten minutes!

MAN: (*Downstairs*) Listen, right? We've got to sort this out while we're here.

(*At the bottom of the stairs in the front hall,* HORTENSE*'s two* BROTHERS *and her* SISTER-IN-LAW *are arguing. A small boy,* HORTENSE*'s nephew, stands with them. Throughout this scene, the camera stays at the top of the stairs, looking down at them – that is, from* HORTENSE*'s implied point of view.*)

SISTER-IN-LAW: Look, basically, right, it's you one here in this massive house.

FIRST BROTHER: Thank you!

SISTER-IN-LAW: It's massive!

FIRST BROTHER: We have got two children, you understand?

SISTER-IN-LAW: And we could 'ave more!

FIRST BROTHER: What?

SISTER-IN-LAW: We wanna 'ave more.

FIRST BROTHER: Listen, right . . . you can't stay here on your own – it's not fair. Is it? I mean, we can sell the house, can't we?

SECOND BROTHER: What?

FIRST BROTHER: Sell the house, and split the money.

SECOND BROTHER: Sell the house? I don't want to sell the house!

SISTER-IN-LAW: Listen, you know what? You could split the whole house in two, right? You could split this into two flats, and it'd still be bigger than our place . . .

FIRST BROTHER: Exactly . . .

SECOND BROTHER: Split it in two? You can't split it in two . . .

(*Upstairs,* HORTENSE *listens. She is both concerned and detached.*)

That night, HORTENSE *sits thoughtfully in her flat. She wears a kerchief on her head. A little later, she folds a printed form, and puts it in an envelope, which she licks.*

The next morning, HORTENSE *posts the letter in a red pillar-box.*

Outside MAURICE's *photographic studio, a Victorian double-fronted shop, bearing the words,* 'MAURICE PURLEY PHOTOGRAPHY'. *People and cars pass by.*

Inside. There now follows a sequence of various people having their photographs taken by MAURICE.

A family group: reluctant HUSBAND, *chirpy* WIFE, *disgruntled overweight teenager, granny on best behaviour.* MAURICE *approaches the* HUSBAND, *and adjusts his tie.*

MAURICE: Now, let's sort your tie out for you, if I may . . . looks just a little bit –

WIFE: Skew-whiff again! (*She giggles.*)

MAURICE: Yes, that's lovely . . .

HUSBAND: Yeah . . .

MAURICE: Wanna 'ave the paper out? (*He removes a newspaper from the* HUSBAND's *pocket.*)

HUSBAND: Yeah, yeah, okay . . .

MAURICE: Cheers.

HUSBAND: Soon as you like . . .

(*For a moment, everybody except the youth talks at once.*)

MAURICE: You ladies look gorgeous – put your hands together, as they are . . . Very nice, okay – here we go . . . (*He disappears behind the camera.*) Put the paper down there. Right, and 'ere we go! Okay? And –

WIFE: Do we say 'cheese', Maurice?

MAURICE: (*Off*) Well, you can if you like, but – you can, you can say 'cheese', you can say whatever you like, but just give me a little bit – (*He snaps.*) That's it!!!

A prize boxer, stripped to the waist, muscles gleaming, and wearing bright red gloves and a famous boxing belt. He snarls ferociously at the camera, arms outstretched. MAURICE *snaps.*

MAURICE: (*Off*) Ah yes! Very sweet . . . (*The boxer leaps around, doing boxing poses and grunts.*) Okay, that's lovely . . .

A NURSE *in uniform poses by an antique chair. She is very nervous.*

MAURICE: (*Off*) So it took you fifteen years, yeah?

NURSE: Yeah.

MAURICE: (*Off*) Did they give you a prize?

9

10

NURSE: No.
MAURICE: (*Off*) Not even a stethoscope or something?
(*She laughs, and* MAURICE *snaps.*)
Lovely!!
(*Her smile is over.*)

A young MOTHER *in white holds her new-born baby.* MAURICE*'s
assistant* JANE *fondles the baby's foot.*
JANE: Little baby . . .
MAURICE: (*Off*) Yeah, that's really lovely – come out, Jane!
MOTHER: I'm so glad he's got his eyes open.
MAURICE: (*Off*) Yeah! That's it, yeah! – and give him a – look
down at him, yeah – lovely! (*He snaps.*)

*A shaggy brown dog lies uneasily on a red plush rostrum. A blonde
middle-aged woman in red joins him, and pushes back his head.*
DOG-OWNER: Are you gonna see that flea collar? Are you gonna
see that?
MAURICE: (*Off*) Don't worry about that – you come out now.
Come out!
DOG-OWNER: Hang on . . . (*She combs the dog's neck busily with
a steel comb.*)
MAURICE: (*Off*) You just come out of the way . . .
DOG-OWNER: That's it. (*She stands up to leave, giving the dog a
final combing.*)
MAURICE: (*Off*) Pop out now –
DOG-OWNER: Yeah! (*She goes.*)
MAURICE: (*Off*) Pop out, and – here we go –
(*Just as* MAURICE *snaps, the* DOG-OWNER*'s hand holding the
comb, appears in the frame.*)
I think we had the comb in there that time!

*A cheerful elderly lady fondles a black-and-white pedigree cat, which
sits on a miniature wicker armchair, round which is tied a large pale
blue silk bow.* MAURICE *snaps.*
MAURICE: (*Off*) Lovely! Very good!
CAT-OWNER: Did he look good?
MAURICE: (*Off*) He does look good.
CAT-OWNER: Oh, good!

MAURICE: (*Off*) So do you!

CAT-OWNER: Yes; yes . . .

> (JANE *creeps in to adjust the silk bow.*)

MAURICE: (*Off*) Thank you very much, Jane, that's lovely . . .

A young Asian MAN *in a suit.* MAURICE *is adjusting his tie.*

MAN: It's for my auntie.

MAURICE: Oh, right? Fond of you, is she?

MAN: No, she's in India.

MAURICE: Oh, right!

MAN: Mm. Time I got married, innit?

MAURICE: Oh, I see. Pick-a-bride time, is it?

> (*He disappears behind the camera, and takes the snap.*)

A MAN *in a tuxedo and a fez. He wears a funny false moustache and eyebrows.*

MAN: I've told you, I don't want flash –

> (MAURICE *snaps him, with flash.*)

Three youngish women do a quasi-provocative pose. Two of them waggle their tongues 'obscenely'.

MAURICE: (*Off*) And – lovely!

> (*He snaps. The trio collapse in uncontrollable mirth.*)

Three identical little girls, obviously triplets, in blue ballet costumes. They pose, holding hands, each pointing her left foot. Their MOTHER *kneels beside one of them, adjusting her tutu.* JANE *is titivating their hair. The lighting behind them looks like two theatrical spotlights.*

MOTHER: I never thought I'd have any. Fertility treatment. It's a miracle.

A small chubby boy with golden locks, a red waistcoat and a tartan bow-tie sits on a miniature red plush chaise-longue, picking his nose. His Irish MOTHER *bustles in, removes the forefinger from the nostril, and leaves.*

MOTHER: Don't do that with your nose –

> (MAURICE *laughs, off.*)

Now stop it! (*She whispers.*) Put it there, that's it.

MAURICE: (*Off*) Hallo, Dominic – look at that lovely cat! Look
over there, look at that cat!
JANE: (*Off*) He's lovely!
(DOMINIC *puts his finger back up his nose.*)
MAURICE: (*Off*) Oh, that's it – let him scratch it first.
MOTHER: (*Off*) No!!

A middle-aged WOMAN *is dressed in 'sexy' lingerie. She is doing a
'provocative' pose, rather awkwardly. A drooping plant sits on top of
a classical column behind her.*
MAURICE: (*Off*) Go on. That's it . . . that's it – lovely!
(*He snaps. The woman giggles self-consciously.*)
WOMAN: I feel so silly!

Five businessmen in suits hold a formal pose.
MAURICE: (*Off*) And lovely, and that's it, and – (*He snaps.*)
Thank you very much!!
(*A bald man looks at his watch.*)

MONICA *is hoovering her downstairs hall. The front door opens just
behind her. It is* MAURICE.
MONICA: What d'you think you're doing?
MAURICE: Sorry.
MONICA: Didn't you hear me?
MAURICE: No. I didn't actually . . . Hiya.
MONICA: What?
MAURICE: (*Going to kiss her*) Hiya.
(*She pushes him off.*)
MONICA: Mind out of the way!
(MAURICE *walks down the hall. He stops in the kitchen
doorway and looks at her for a moment. Then he goes to the
fridge, opens it, and takes out a previously opened bottle of white
wine. He goes back to the doorway, holding the wine bottle.*)
MAURICE: D'you want a drink?
(MONICA *turns off the hoover.*)
MONICA: What? If I want a drink, I'll get it myself, thank you!
(*She unplugs the hoover.* MAURICE *goes back towards the
fridge, and puts down the bottle on a worktop. He pauses for a
moment, and sighs. Then he goes back to the doorway, and*

looks at MONICA *as she feeds the cable into the hoover. This finished, she comes into the kitchen.*)

Since when was hoovering a spectator sport?

(*She goes to the fridge, and takes out a bottle of milk.* MAURICE *gets a wine glass out of a cupboard.*)

Can I have a glass, too, please?

MAURICE: I'm sorry, I thought you didn't want any.

MONICA: I've changed my mind – I'm 'avin' milk.

MAURICE: (*Giving her glass*) There you go.

MONICA: Not in a wine glass – give me a highball –

MAURICE: (*At same time*) Okay –

MONICA: You don't put milk in a wine glass!

(*He gets out a highball.*)

MAURICE: (*Giving her glass*) There you go.

MONICA: Thank you! (*She pours the milk.*)

MAURICE: That'll do you good!

MONICA: Meanin'?

MAURICE: Nothing.

Moments later. MONICA *opens the oven, and looks into it. It is empty. She sighs.*

MAURICE: Had a good day?

MONICA: Scintillating! (*She slams the oven door, then opens and slams shut the microwave door. Then, as she sits at the table:*) I suppose you'll be starvin', as usual?!

(*She swigs the milk in one go.* MAURICE *joins her at the table.*)

MAURICE: I'm a little bit peckish, yeah . . .

(MONICA *slams down her empty glass on the table.*)

D'you want me to do something?

MONICA: Like what?!

MAURICE: Anything you like.

MONICA: No, I bloody well wouldn't!

MAURICE: Fair enough.

MONICA: (*Getting up*) Oh, all right, then.

(*She gets up and goes round the kitchen.*) There's the fridge! (*She opens and shuts it.*) Freezer! (*She opens and shuts it.*) There's the hob! (*She points to it.*) There's the recipe books! (*Points.*) Help yourself! (*She closes the patio door.*) And don't make a mess!

(*She goes into the hall, and puts away the hoover in a cupboard under the stairs.* MAURICE *looks worried.* MONICA *comes to the kitchen door. Then, a touch more reasonably:*)
Unless you fancy a takeaway?
(MAURICE *smiles slightly. For a moment,* MONICA *looks as though she is about to share this, but instead she breaks down in tears.* MAURICE *looks at her, a combination of concern and sympathy, and she rushes out of the room, slamming the door behind her.*)

And now MAURICE *takes some more studio portraits.*

   An aggressive-looking young punk WOMAN GRADUATE, *wearing her mortarboard and robes, and holding a scroll, leans on the classical column, on top of which is a pile of old leather-bound books.*
MAURICE: (*Off*) You're not going to smile, are you?
GRADUATE: (*Sulkily*) No!
MAURICE: (*Off*) Okay. It's a free world . . . (*He snaps.*)

A young couple, smartly dressed. The man sits, grinning deliriously. The woman stands behind him with her hands on his shoulder. She looks extremely fed up.
MAURICE: (*Off*) Now you're under no obligation, but you can if

you want give me a lovely big SMILE . . . and – (*He snaps.*) – thank you.

An uneasy black woman, and an older white man, also uneasy. She is smiling, and he is trying to, with some reservations.
MAURICE: (*Off*) Oh, go on, come on, lovely! (*He snaps.*)

A very OLD LADY *sits, looking very cross. A smiling middle-aged* WOMAN *stands beside her with her hands on the* OLD LADY's *shoulder.*
MAURICE: (*Off*) And you're under no obligation to, but you can smile if you like – yes, thank you!! (*He snaps.*)
YOUNGER WOMAN: Did you smile, Mother?
OLD LADY: No!

A very jolly couple in their early forties, informally dressed. They obviously have a great sense of fun. Both have protruding teeth. They sit, side by side, smiling and giggling.
MAURICE: (*Off*) That's it, to me, that's it – now look at each other!
    (*They do so.* MAURICE *snaps. They laugh uproariously and endlessly as* MAURICE *prompts them from behind the camera, and snaps them.*)

MONICA *is in her bathroom. She sits on the toilet. From a basket on her knees, she takes a Tampax out of its packet. Then she puts the basket on the floor. She is in some pain.*

A little later, we see, through an upstairs window, MAURICE's *car pulling into the drive.*

Now MAURICE *is filling a rubber hot-water bottle from the bath tap.*
MONICA *is lying in bed. Daylight.*
MONICA: (*Calling through*) Don't forget to burp it properly!
    (MAURICE *screws in the bottle top, and walks into the adjacent bedroom.*)
MAURICE: Give it a drop of gripe-water. We used to pour it down Roxanne by the gallon. (*He rests the bottle on his shoulder, and pats it like a baby.*) She farted like a trooper.

MONICA: Runs in the family.

(MAURICE *kneels on the bed and gives* MONICA *the bottle.*)

MAURICE: Would Madame care to test the temperature?

MONICA: I'm sure it'll be fine – thanks.

(*She puts it under the duvet.* MAURICE *sits at the end of the brass four-poster bed, facing* MONICA.)

MAURICE: Been bad, has it?

MONICA: It eased off at lunchtime. Managed a couple of crackers.

(MAURICE *chuckles.*)

MAURICE: Unpredictable, isn't it?

MONICA: No, it's not unpredictable.

MAURICE: You've drawn the short straw, mate.

MONICA: You're telling me. I wish it was unpredictable. (*Pause.*) What are you going to have for your tea?

MAURICE: D'you know what I really fancy?

MONICA: What?

MAURICE: A steak.

MONICA: You're not havin' any steak in this house.

MAURICE: Don't worry about me.

MONICA: You'll be keeling over with a heart attack.

MAURICE: I'll do meself something later.

MONICA: There's a chicken Kiev in the freezer.

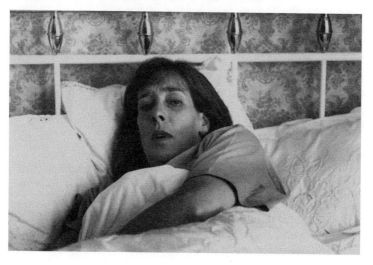

MAURICE: Be a bit cold, wouldn't it?
    (MONICA *chortles.*)
    Anyway, I'm on a diet. (*He pats his belly.*)
MONICA: (*Smiling*) You're disgustin'!

*Another session in the studio. A respectable couple in their thirties
pose formally. The* MAN *stands slightly behind the* WOMAN, *one
hand on her shoulder, the other holding her hand.*
MAURICE: (*Off*) Okay, that's very good; and we can see the ring
    perfectly. All right – now, sir, if you can just bring your
    chin up –
    (*As the man does so, the woman looks up at him.*)
WOMAN: (*Quietly*) Sorry, sorry . . . Listen, you, em – will you
    take your glasses off . . .?
MAN: I don't wanna take my glasses off!
    (*Pause.*)
WOMAN: (*Whispering*) Go on, take them off.
    (*He removes them, with an air of long-suffering, and puts them
    in his pocket.*)
MAURICE: (*Off*) It doesn't matter – keep them on . . .
MAN: That's all right.
WOMAN: No, he looks better without them . . .
MAN: It's what I look like, okay?

MAURICE: (*Off*) Right, okay – and to me . . .

MAN: One minute, please – will you take the cross out, please?

WOMAN: Mm?

MAN: Take the cross out! It's a gift – take it out.

(*She is wearing a crucifix necklace. She pulls the cross out from under her blouse.*)

WOMAN: I just think it looks awful.

MAN: It doesn't look awful – it looks awful 'cos it's not gold. I told you to buy gold.

MAURICE: (*Off*) Okay, right –

(*The couple now exchange angry words in Greek.*)

Okay, and to me – yeah, right, that's lovely – now, d'you want to look happy or sad, I don't mind – whatever you want . . .

(*They smile.*)

Ah, look at you, and keep yer – and look at me, and LOVELY!

(*A flash, and* MAURICE *has captured their Happy Moment; the photograph over, they dissolve into an embarrassed pause.*)

HORTENSE *walks up the steps to her front door, and lets herself in. A large brown envelope is lying on the mat. She picks it up. She enters her own flat, and opens the envelope as she climbs the stairs. She stops to read it at the top.*

Next day, in the examining room at work. HORTENSE *is on the phone.*

HORTENSE: Hello, my name is Hortense Cumberbatch . . . I got your letter – hi!

(*Pause.*)

Oh, right . . . Tuesday.

Tuesday. HORTENSE *is sitting waiting in a public building. Posters, noticeboards, a man sitting waiting along a corridor. A phone rings. A* RECEPTIONIST *stands up into view behind a hatch.*

RECEPTIONIST: Hello?

(*A small efficient-looking* WOMAN *in her late thirties rushes down the stairs. She carries a shoulder-bag and a folder. She shakes* HORTENSE *by the hand.*)

WOMAN: Hortense? Hallo – Jenny Ford. Nice to meet you.

HORTENSE: Oh, hi . . .

JENNY: Come this way.

> (*She sets off down a corridor.* HORTENSE *gets up and follows her.*)

How are you, all right?

HORTENSE: Fine, thank you.

JENNY: Good. (*She opens a door and leads* HORTENSE *into a room at the end of the corridor.*) Sorry about this prison cell – we've been banging on about it for years, but there you go. Have a seat, make yourself at home.

> (*She closes the door.* HORTENSE *sits down. The room is bare and institutional. The walls are covered with notices and posters about Violence, Rights, AIDS, etc. A single toy plastic bus sits on the windowsill.* JENNY *sits opposite* HORTENSE.)

Now, before we go any further, have you got any ID? Passport, driving licence?

HORTENSE: Oh, yeah.

JENNY: You'll have to get used to all this red tape – would you like a Rolo?

HORTENSE: (*Searching her bag*) No, thank you.

JENNY: Are you sure?

HORTENSE: Yeah. (*She pulls out her driving licence, and hands it over.*) There you go.

> (JENNY *has popped a Rolo into her mouth. She takes the licence.*)

JENNY: Have a shufti . . . (*She examines it.*) That's great, Hortense. Thanks. (*She returns it.*)

HORTENSE: Thank you.

JENNY: You on your lunch break?

HORTENSE: Yeah, an extended one.

JENNY: Have you 'ad any lunch?

HORTENSE: No, not yet.

JENNY: No, me neither. So what d'you do?

HORTENSE: I'm an optometrist.

JENNY: Oh, really? Oh, God . . . (*She laughs drily.*) It's one of those things you keep putting off and putting off, isn't it? (HORTENSE *smiles politely.*)

I've got to the stage with the *Guardian* crossword where

I'm going like this. (*She demonstrates squinting.*) So I think the time has come, don't you? I'll 'ave to pop in, you can give me a test. Where d'you live?

HORTENSE: Kilburn.

JENNY: Right, right. In a flat?

HORTENSE: Yes.

JENNY: D'you share?

HORTENSE: No, I live on my own.

JENNY: Oh, right. I lived on my own, for about six years – before I was married. 'T's all right, isn't it? (*She laughs.*)

HORTENSE: Yeah.

JENNY: Right, Hortense. Let's talk a little bit about you, shall we? Now, obviously, you've been giving a great deal of thought to things, and you've come to a decision, which is good. But, for me, the question is: why now?

HORTENSE: I just feel that it's the right time, that's all.

JENNY: Right, right. Are you thinking about getting married?

HORTENSE: No.

JENNY: D'you have children?

HORTENSE: No.

JENNY: Are you thinking about having children?

HORTENSE: (*Laughing*) No.

JENNY: 'T's fair enough. Are you sharing this with your parents? Do they know that you're here today? How do they feel about it?

HORTENSE: They're both dead, actually.

JENNY: Oh, right.

HORTENSE: Er . . . Mum died . . . two months ago now . . .

JENNY: Oh, that is recent – I'm sorry to hear that. Was it sudden?

HORTENSE: Yeah.

JENNY: Perhaps that's what's made you start on this?

HORTENSE: I don't know.

JENNY: It's possible.

HORTENSE: Well, I'm not trying to replace her; she's irreplaceable – well, they both are.

JENNY: No – of course; of course. And when you were growin' up, was it – was it a happy environment?

HORTENSE: Yes, very.

JENNY: Oh, good, good, and did you, em . . . were you able to
. . .to discuss the fact that you'd been –
HORTENSE: No, it was never really an issue.
JENNY: Right, right. So you've only just found out?
HORTENSE: Oh, no. They told me when I was little.
JENNY: Oh, good, good. And d'you remember how you felt
about that?
HORTENSE: (*Amused*) Well, it's not exactly something you
forget, is it?
JENNY: No, no . . . (*Returning* HORTENSE*'s amusement.*) I'm
sure it isn't.
(*Pause.*)
So how did you feel?
HORTENSE: Well . . . we all just got on with it as a family, d'you
know what I mean?
JENNY: Yeah. Perhaps you should've discussed it.
HORTENSE: My parents loved me, and that's all that matters.
Isn't it?
JENNY: Yeah, yeah. So, now that we've got you here, what are
your expectations?
HORTENSE: Basically . . . I just want to know.
JENNY: Yeah, yeah – course you do. Let me share something
with you, Hortense. Somewhere out there, and we don't
know where, is your birth mother. Now . . . she's probably
married. Perhaps not. She may have other children; she
might be dead. She may even be in Australia or
somewhere, we just don't know, but what we do know is
. . . that, at the time she gave you up for adoption, she was
under the impression that she would probably never see
you again. Now, as I know you're very well aware, the law
has changed since then, and you are now legally entitled to
seek your birth mother out. But the snag is . . . she may
not want to see you. So I don't want you to raise your
hopes too high at this stage.
HORTENSE: Sure.
JENNY: Okay?
(HORTENSE *nods.*)
Have a look at this . . . (*She gives* HORTENSE *the folder.*)
HORTENSE: What is it?

JENNY: It's all about you.

  (*Pause.*)

  I'll tell you what. (*She picks up her bag.*) I'll leave it with you, and I'll pop back in a few minutes. (*She gets up and touches* HORTENSE *gently.*) Can I get you anything?

HORTENSE: No. Thank you.

  (JENNY *leaves the room, closing the door behind her.* HORTENSE *watches her go. Then she opens the folder, and takes out a sheaf of assorted pieces of paper. She looks through them. They include some headed, 'The National Adoption Society'. She is bewildered, shocked, shaken. Tears well in her eyes.*

  After a while, JENNY *can be seen through a window in the door. She opens the door sensitively, but the hinges creak, and she winces as she shuts it. She joins* HORTENSE, *and for a moment rubs her back gently.*)

JENNY: How're you doing – all right?

  (*She produces a small packet of paper tissues from her bag, and holds one out for* HORTENSE, *who takes it.*)

HORTENSE: Thank you. (*She blows her nose.*) Cynthia Rose Purley. That's her.

JENNY: Cynthia Rose. That's a nice name, isn't it?

HORTENSE: That's her signature.

JENNY: Mm – hm. That feels strange?

(HORTENSE *can't reply. Then* . . .)

HORTENSE: Elizabeth. That's my middle name. They must a' kept it.

JENNY: Well . . . that would be your birth name – you see: Elizabeth Purley.

(*Pause.* HORTENSE *sighs, and wipes her nose.*)

HORTENSE: Listen . . . Is there any way I could get a copy of these?

JENNY: No – those are the originals, and they're yours to keep. That's your right, under the 1975 Act – I've made copies upstairs. (*She has brought back with her a new large brown envelope, and she takes the sheaf of documents from* HORTENSE.) Pop those in here . . . for you. (*She does so, and swaps the envelope for the empty folder.*) So . . . what we need to do now is . . . you go away, and 'ave a think. And when the time's right, and not before – you know, it's very much in your own time . . . come back to me, if that's what you want, and we'll get the ball rolling. Now, it can be a very . . . long-winded process, and there's no two ways about it, it's a very traumatic journey we're embarkin' on; and there may be other people's feelings to consider, too. So I'll wait to hear from you, okay? Now, you could decide to trace your birth mother by yourself . . . if you wanted, but I wouldn't advise it – we're a professional service . . . (*She looks at her watch, and glances quickly over her shoulder through the window in the door.*) And we know how to handle these things. So, I think you should take advantage of us.

HORTENSE *is in her car, studying one of the documents. Suddenly, something catches her eye.*

A few minutes later, JENNY *rushes out of the Social Services building. She meets* HORTENSE.

HORTENSE: Hello . . .

JENNY: (*Without stopping*) Oh, you're back – hello!

HORTENSE: I think I've found a mistake.

JENNY: I'm sorry, Hortense, I can't stop, I –

24

HORTENSE: Look, it says she's white.

JENNY: (*Stopping*) Sorry? (*She joins* HORTENSE, *and looks at the document.*)

HORTENSE: 'Mother – white.'

JENNY: Well . . . it's perfectly feasible that your mother was white, isn't it?

(HORTENSE *doesn't reply.* JENNY *starts to leave.*)

Look – I'm sorry, Hortense, really, I've got to go – I'm on an emergency case.

HORTENSE: Yes, but could this be a mistake?

(JENNY *stops for a moment.*)

JENNY: I very much doubt it.

(*Pause.*)

Look, give me a ring in the morning, and we'll have a talk then – okay? I'm sorry.

(*She rushes off.* HORTENSE *stands looking at the papers. It is a bright, sunny day.*)

On the same sunny day, CYNTHIA *and* ROXANNE *are sitting in their living-room.* CYNTHIA *has a tumbler of whisky in her hand.* ROXANNE *is replacing the batteries in her Walkman.* CYNTHIA *puts a bare foot on the coffee table.*

CYNTHIA: Look at that. (*She puts the other foot alongside the first; she wears a slipper on this one.*) Legs like a teenager.

ROXANNE: D'you 'ave to?

CYNTHIA: You'd like a pair like that.

ROXANNE: What for?

CYNTHIA: I'm known for my legs. If you've got it, flaunt it. (*She sips the whisky.*) You goin' out?

ROXANNE: Course I ain't.

(*There is a knock at the front door.*)

CYNTHIA: 'Oo's that?

ROXANNE: Well, I don't know.

(*She gets up and goes out.* CYNTHIA *puts on her other slipper.*)

CYNTHIA: If it's what'sername, you can ask 'er to come in.

(*In the hall,* ROXANNE *is approaching the front door.*)

ROXANNE: I don't even know 'oo it is yet!

(*She opens the door to reveal a worried-looking young* MAN, *panting hard and wearing a sweatshirt and a leather jacket.*)

25

What're you doin' 'ere?

MAN: Just come to see yer.

ROXANNE: Well, you can't come in – my mum's 'ere. (*She shuts the door.*)

CYNTHIA: (*Off*) 'Oo is it?

ROXANNE: I'm goin' out.

(*She gets her coat from the hall.* CYNTHIA *appears behind her.* ROXANNE *opens the door. The* MAN *is still there.*)

CYNTHIA: (*To* MAN) 'Ello . . .

(*The* MAN *follows* ROXANNE, *who has marched off down the street.* CYNTHIA *shouts after her.*)

You all right, sweet'eart?

(ROXANNE *stops for a moment.*)

ROXANNE: Would you get inside?

(*She continues down the street, still followed by the* MAN, *who has a rather stiff gait. As they disappear round the corner, he looks at* CYNTHIA. *Perplexed, she glances round the street, then goes back into the house.*)

ROXANNE *is with* PAUL (*for that is the* MAN's *name*) *in his bed-sit. She surveys the cooker and the sink.*

ROXANNE: Nothing's changed much.

PAUL: No.

ROXANNE: Ain't yer mum been round, lookin' after yer?

PAUL: She came round Sunday, after Mass.

ROXANNE: Didn't take yer long to mess it up again!

PAUL: She's layin' off me a bit now, though.

ROXANNE: I should think so, too, at your age.

PAUL: Yeah.

ROXANNE: She should 'ave a word with my mum.

(*She joins him on the sofa. He is smoking.*)

I bet she misses you, though.

PAUL: Fuckin' . . . do without it altogether, I tell you.

ROXANNE: Yeah, I know what you mean; you an' me, mate, we're better off without 'em. (*She lights a cigarette.*)

PAUL: Look . . . sorry about . . . y'know.

ROXANNE: So you should be. Don't get all serious on me, Paul!

PAUL: No, no . . . I ain't.

ROXANNE: Yes, you are, you fool!

PAUL: Just missed yer.

ROXANNE: 'Ow much?

PAUL: A lot.

ROXANNE: Just a lot?

PAUL: No! Yeah . . .

ROXANNE: Well, I might've missed you a bit. No, I've been goin' out o' me 'ead.

PAUL: Same as that.

(*Pause. Slowly they move to kiss,* PAUL *breathing heavily.* ROXANNE *pulls away suddenly.*)

ROXANNE: Just so's you know, I ain't stayin' the night – not every time I come round. And I weren't in a strop before – I was just speakin' my mind. All right?

PAUL: (*Inaudible*) Yeah.

ROXANNE: Now give us a snog.

(*They both smile, and get down to some serious snogging.*)

That night. CYNTHIA *is alone in her bedroom. She is drunk. She is wearing a low-cut nightdress. She stands in front of the mirror. She rubs cold cream into her face. Then she feels her breasts sensuously.*

At the same moment, HORTENSE *sits on her bed, studying the documents. She is crying.*

Next day. A busy London street. HORTENSE *walks round the corner and enters another public building. A sign by the door says, 'Office of Population Censuses and Surveys'. This is St Catherine's House in the Aldwych.*

Inside, HORTENSE *passes another pair of signs, 'Births 1974 to 1983' and 'Births 1964 to 1973'. She is holding another official form. She looks along a long line of large red leather-bound volumes. She finds the one she's looking for, takes it out, and carries it to a long desk. Other youngish people are browsing similar volumes. She eventually finds the information she seeks, and starts to fill out the form.*

A little later, HORTENSE *is at the window of a pay counter. A long queue is in the background. The* CASHIER *is a bald man with glasses.*

CASHIER: Hello, good afternoon.

HORTENSE: Hello.

CASHIER: Thank you very much indeed. (*He checks her paperwork.*) Right that's fine – is that, er, to post, or collect?

HORTENSE: Collect, please.

CASHIER: Collect. Thanks very much. That's six pounds, please, madam.

HORTENSE: Six . . . (*She sorts out the money.*)

That evening, another bright summer's one, HORTENSE *and her friend* DIONNE *are sitting at* HORTENSE*'s kitchen table. They have had supper, and are sipping white wine. They are looking reflective.*

DIONNE: I saw 'er, you know?

HORTENSE: Did yer?

DIONNE: Yeah. Eight o'clock in the morning, she's down Harlesden, buyin' her yam and banana; she says like, 'You got a boyfriend yet, Dionne?' (*She laughs.*)

HORTENSE: Nearly everyone 'oo went to the funeral reckoned they'd seen 'er, and she'd given then some kind of sign. (*Ancient West Indian lady's voice:*) 'Me see your mudder two days before she dead, an' she hol' on to me an' look in me eye as if she did know.'
(*They both laugh. Then* HORTENSE *becomes reflective again.*)
I mean, if she knew, I wish she'd told us.

DIONNE: You're getting better, though.

HORTENSE: It's a nice day.

DIONNE: (*Looking out of window*) Yeah.
(*Pause.*)

HORTENSE: I dunno. My 'ead can't contain it all – it's too soon. There's nothing rational about grief. Maybe you're crying for yourself.

DIONNE: Have you been out much?

HORTENSE: No, I can't. Some days . . . I'm completely vulnerable – I can feel everything; other days, I'm numb.

DIONNE: You wanna come out with me?

HORTENSE: No! I've got stuff to sort out.

DIONNE: What?

HORTENSE: Life.

DIONNE: Look, if there's anything I can do . . .

HORTENSE: No – thanks. I'll be all right.

DIONNE: Have you heard from Bernard?

HORTENSE: No. Yes! He sent a sympathy card.

DIONNE: Did he?

HORTENSE: Which I thought was a very nice thing to do.

DIONNE: Mm.

>(HORTENSE *makes a funny, grotesque face, a sort of pouting kiss, presumably some private reference to Bernard.* DIONNE *imitates this, and they both burst into naughty, conspiratorial laughter.*)

>I did something really bad.

HORTENSE: Oh, no, I don't think I can deal with no confessions.

DIONNE: Cleanse my soul!

HORTENSE: Mm – mm!

DIONNE: I did the do!

HORTENSE: Do it!

DIONNE: Did the deed!

HORTENSE: Did it!

DIONNE: With a complete stranger.

HORTENSE: No – who?

DIONNE: Dunno. (*She giggles.*)

HORTENSE: Well, what did 'e look like?

DIONNE: Dunno. 'E was in advertising.

HORTENSE: (*West Indian accent*) Oh, Lard!

(*They laugh.* HORTENSE *buries her head in her arm. Normal voice:*)

Did you use a condom?

DIONNE: Yes.

HORTENSE: Did you use two?

DIONNE: Yes.

HORTENSE: One on top of the other?

DIONNE: One after the other.

HORTENSE: Oh, God!

DIONNE: (*Laughing*) D'you despair of me?

HORTENSE: (*Looking at her*) No.

DIONNE: Yes, you do.

HORTENSE: I don't. Did you 'ave a good time?

DIONNE: Yeah.

HORTENSE: That's all that matters, then, innit?

DIONNE: Yeah.

(*She smiles, and sips some wine.* HORTENSE *laughs quietly.*)

Later. They are relaxing in HORTENSE*'s living-room.* HORTENSE *is lying on her sofa.* DIONNE *is sitting on the floor, leaning against the sofa with her back to* HORTENSE. *She sips wine occasionally.*

HORTENSE: I liked my mum as a person, but I didn't know 'er. I wish I'd known 'er.

DIONNE: She loved you.

HORTENSE: Yeah, I know, but that's not in debate, is it?

DIONNE: My mum, she resents me.

HORTENSE: She kept you. She fed you, she clothed you . . . she didn't give you away! She could've.

DIONNE: I wish she 'ad.

HORTENSE: No, you don't. The thing is, they're so secretive; it's that back-home thing – y'know: 'Come out, big people are talkin'!' That sort of vibe. So you don't pursue things . . . because you're brought up not to.

DIONNE: I just let 'em get on with it.

HORTENSE: All I seem to do is think about things I wish I could've asked her.

31

DIONNE: Like what?

(*Pause.*)

HORTENSE: I dunno. There's stuff I wish I knew.

DIONNE: There's stuff I wish I didn't know.

HORTENSE: No. If you knew you had a limited amount of time, you'd sort it out, you'd ask your mum questions . . . regardless of whether she got vex. Like . . . I dunno, what 'appened between her and your dad, for example.

DIONNE: No! She ain't made no effort for me, so why should I be interested in 'er? And where's my dad, anyway? I don't want to 'ear her and Norbert 'avin' it off; I don't want 'er to know 'oo I'm 'avin it off with; and I don't want 'er to see me drunk. I don't want 'er to know nothin' about me.

HORTENSE: Maybe that's because you're frightened that when you look at 'er, you can see yourself in twenty years' time.

DIONNE: Please!

HORTENSE: We choose our parents.

DIONNE: 'Ow d'you mean?

HORTENSE: We choose the parents in this life that can teach us something; so that when we go into the next life, we get it right.

DIONNE: Zhoop! (*As she says this, she makes a gesture – like a plane flying over – that means, 'That went right over my head.'*)

HORTENSE: Course, sometimes it don't work, does it?

Daylight. The optometrist's shop. HORTENSE *comes out of the back room, and stops to speak to the senior* OPTOMETRIST, *an older woman, who is wearing a white coat, and working at a desk.*

HORTENSE: I'm going to pop out for a couple of hours.

OPTOMETRIST: What time will you be back?

HORTENSE: Four-thirty.

OPTOMETRIST: Okay. Have fun.

HORTENSE: Thanks. (*On the way out of the shop she stops to speak to the junior* OPTICIAN *we met in an earlier scene, and who is serving a customer.* HORTENSE *gives her a small slip of paper.*) Sorry to interrupt. Could you get me a few of these things in?

OPTICIAN: Right.

HORTENSE: I'm a bit low.

OPTICIAN: I'll give 'em a ring.
(HORTENSE *leaves.*)

Later. St Catherine's House. HORTENSE *comes out of the swing doors with a document. She studies it for a few moments. Then she walks off.*

She sits in her car, examining this latest document. We see it in close-up. It is her Birth Certificate. We can clearly read, 'C. R. Purley', and an address, '76 Quilter Street'. HORTENSE *opens the glove compartment and takes out a copy of* The London A to Z. *She flicks through it, running her finger down the index; then she looks for a map page . . .*
HORTENSE: Seventy-nine . . .

HORTENSE *weaves through the London traffic in her car.*
    Now she turns into a street of small Victorian terraced houses with no front gardens. A sign says 'Quilter Street'. She slows down, looking for the house in question. When she finds it, she stops for a few moments, and has a look. She sighs. Then she drives off.

Later the same afternoon. Quilter Street. MAURICE *has just parked his car, and is taking his metal case out of the boot. An elderly pot-bellied man, stripped to the waist, stands watching him from a doorway further down the street.* MAURICE *locks the boot, and walks to* CYNTHIA'S *front door. He knocks. Then he looks around for a while.* CYNTHIA *opens the door. She is eating a sandwich. She looks shocked and amazed.*
MAURICE: Hullo.
CYNTHIA: Bloody 'ell! What're you doin' 'ere?
MAURICE: Thought I'd come and see yer.
CYNTHIA: Where's Monica?
MAURICE: She's at home, I think. (*He chuckles.*) Are you going to let me in, then?
CYNTHIA: Yeah – course.
        (*She backs inside.* MAURICE *follows her in, and closes the door. They go into the kitchen.*)
        D'you wanna cup o' tea?
MAURICE: Yes, please!

33

(*He takes off his jacket and hangs it up.* CYNTHIA *gets a toilet-roll from the scullery.*)
You all right, then?

CYNTHIA: (*Giving him toilet-roll*) Smashin'. You been working down this way?

MAURICE: Yeah, back o' Tower Bridge. (*He goes out to the garden.*)

CYNTHIA: If I'd known you was comin', I'd 'ave warmed up the seat.

MAURICE: (*Outside*) It's warm enough, I should think.

A few minutes later. CYNTHIA *comes out into the garden, and stops by an old disused mangle. She is smoking a cigarette.*

CYNTHIA: Does Monica know you've come round 'ere?

MAURICE: (*From inside the outside lavatory*) No, I didn't know I was coming meself.

CYNTHIA: She's okay, then?

MAURICE: Yeah, she's fine. She's busy with the house.

CYNTHIA: What doin'? I thought it was supposed to be a new 'ouse, you said.

MAURICE: Stencilling.

CYNTHIA: What, drawin'?

(*We see* MAURICE *over the top of the door.*)

MAURICE: No, stencils, on the wall. Decoratin'. You must've seen it in magazines. It's very effective.

(CYNTHIA *looks displeased. She goes back into the house.* MAURICE *is unaware of this.*)
Roxanne not in, then?

A few minutes later, in the kitchen, MAURICE *is wiping his hands on a towel.* CYNTHIA *is sitting at the table.*

CYNTHIA: She's got some bloke in tow.

MAURICE: Has she?

CYNTHIA: Shifty-lookin' bleeder. Walks like a crab.

(MAURICE *chuckles, and comes to join her at the table.*)
Your tea's there.

MAURICE: Ta.

CYNTHIA: D'you wanna sandwich?

MAURICE: (*Sitting*) No, thanks. Is that all you're 'avin'?

34

CYNTHIA: I only see 'er first thing in the morning – she comes in, grunts, then buggers off to work.

MAURICE: You should be glad she's got a feller.

CYNTHIA: I am glad, Maurice – I wan' 'er to be 'appy! But I'd like 'er to bring 'im round – see 'oo's she's knockin' about with.

MAURICE: Just give 'er a bit of time.

CYNTHIA: You used to bring your girlfriends 'ome. Front of the telly, laugh, drink . . . You didn't mind me sittin' there, did yer?

(MAURICE *chuckles reminiscently*.)

What's 'er name? Never stopped talkin'.

MAURICE: Tina.

CYNTHIA: Tina. Then the other one, wouldn't open 'er mouth.

(*Pause.*)

MAURICE: Maxine.

CYNTHIA: That's it. Dad liked her, didn' 'e?

(MAURICE *smiles*.)

Nice thighs.

MAURICE: So how's work, then? Are you still at the same place?

CYNTHIA: Yeah. I've gotta get 'er something for 'er birthday – it's 'er twenny-first, Maurice!

MAURICE: August the seventh.

CYNTHIA: I dunno what she wants . . . 'part from me under a bus.

MAURICE: That's silly talk.

CYNTHIA: Me 'ead in the oven.

MAURICE: When are you gonna come and see us, then?

CYNTHIA: Eh?

MAURICE: You know – a bit of a get-together. Come on Roxanne's birthday – we'll have some champagne.

CYNTHIA: What about Monica?

MAURICE: (*Laughing*) She'll be there.

CYNTHIA: Won't she mind?

MAURICE: No. It's her idea, actually.

CYNTHIA: Oh . . .

MAURICE: How d'you fancy a barbecue?

CYNTHIA: If you like.

MAURICE: Anyway, it's about time you saw the house.

35

CYNTHIA: Thought you was never gonna ask.

MAURICE: Well, I'm asking you now.

CYNTHIA: You've been there nearly a twelve-month!

MAURICE: Tell Roxanne. She might not want to come.

CYNTHIA: She'll say no, just to spite me.

MAURICE: Yeah, well, I demand 'er presence. Tell 'er.

CYNTHIA: What if she wants to bring 'im?

MAURICE: Has he got a job, this bloke?

CYNTHIA: Scaffoldin', she says.

MAURICE: Oh. It's very well paid.

CYNTHIA: Is it?

MAURICE: Yep. (*He reflects.*) Twenty-one . . .

CYNTHIA: I can't believe it, Maurice. I was carryin' 'er when I
was twenny-one, wa'n' I? (*She smiles.*) You was good with
nappies.

MAURICE: (*Laughing*) Those safety-pins, though!

CYNTHIA: Never stabbed 'er, though, did you, darlin'?

MAURICE: Stabbed meself a couple o' times.

CYNTHIA: Seventeen, wa'n't yer?

(*Pause.*)

MAURICE: I was.

(*They share unspoken memories.*)

At this very moment, HORTENSE, *in her flat, looks at a small black
notebook. The phone is on her lap. She picks up the receiver, as if to
make a call. She hesitates for a while. Then she hangs up, shaking
her head. After a few moments' thought, she closes the notebook, and
sighs.*

Meanwhile, MAURICE *is perched on the armchair in* CYNTHIA's
living-room. He is holding his mug of tea. CYNTHIA *comes in.*

MAURICE: Place is still standing, then?

CYNTHIA: Not for much longer – you should see Dad's room.

MAURICE: What's up with it?

CYNTHIA: It's like the Niagara Falls up there.

MAURICE: What, 's it got a leak?

CYNTHIA: Yeah. Only when it's rainin'.

MAURICE: I'll 'ave a look.

(*He finishes his tea, puts down the mug, gets up, looks at his
watch, and leaves the room.* CYNTHIA *follows him.*)

CYNTHIA: Nice to 'ave a man about the place. (*She follows* MAURICE *upstairs.*) I wish I'd known you was comin'.

Minutes later, MAURICE *is standing on his parents' bed next to a plastic bowl. He is testing the wall, which has a large leak-stain.* CYNTHIA *is leaning on the door.*

MAURICE: It's dry at the moment.

CYNTHIA: The 'ole lot's going to come down.

    (MAURICE *prods a hole in the ceiling.*)

MAURICE: Yeah, it does look a bit dodgy, I'll have to admit. Are you up to date on the rent?

CYNTHIA: Course I am!

MAURICE: Well, give him a ring, get him to do something about it – it's his responsibility.

CYNTHIA: Don't be daft, Maurice, 'e don't give a toss, does 'e?

MAURICE: Well, get someone to look at it . . . I'll pay.

    (*He gets off the bed, and crosses the room.* CYNTHIA *still holds on to the door.*)

    Look at all this junk. What're you going to do with it?

    (*Pause.* CYNTHIA *turns away.*)

CYNTHIA: Give us a cuddle, Maurice . . . please sweet'eart!!

    (*She rushes across the room, throws her arms round him, and hugs him tightly. She cries into his shoulder. He does not*

respond easily; slowly, awkwardly and undemonstratively, he
manages to hold her. She speaks through her tears.)
Why have you left it so bloody long?
MAURICE: You know . . . it's, it's work, and . . .
CYNTHIA: There's nothing the matter with your dialling finger!
MAURICE: You can ring *me*!
CYNTHIA: You're always too busy, in't yer?
(*She sobs. He tries to detach her.*)
MAURICE: Look, em . . . look . . . sit, sit yourself down –
CYNTHIA: You're the only one I've got, Maurice. (*Sobbing.*)
You love me, don't yer? Hold me tight, Maurice, please!
(*He does so.*)
Sorry, darlin'! (*She breaks down, a long sobbing cry. When
this eventually subsides, she rests on his chest, a sort of laughter
now joining the tears.*) My little brother! Look at yer! (*She
pats his tummy.*) There's the good life for yer!!
(*He almost laughs. She hugs his head, kisses his face, and
strokes his beard.*)
When are you gonna shave, eh?
(*Another slight chortle from* MAURICE.)
Slap yer arse!
(*She does so, three jokey little smacks. Pause. She rubs his
chest.*)

MAURICE: Why don't you chuck it all out, eh? I mean, look at it
. . . (*He goes to the cluttered dressing-table, and picks up an old
hairbrush.*) Some of it hasn't been touched since Mum
died.

CYNTHIA: Can you use anything, Maurice, in yer new 'ouse?
Fill a space . . .

MAURICE: No, thanks.

CYNTHIA: Thought I might move in 'ere. Front view. See the
world go by.

(MAURICE *goes to the mantelpiece, and flicks the switch of an
old bulbless lamp.* CYNTHIA *watches him for a moment. Then
she looks round the room.*)

Remember this? (*She picks up a well-worn artificial
Christmas tree.*)

MAURICE: Yeah.

CYNTHIA: That's no use to you, is it?

MAURICE: (*Smiling*) I don't think so.

CYNTHIA: You ain't gonna make me an auntie now, are yer?
Sweet'eart?

(*Pause.* MAURICE *is overcome.*)

MAURICE: Listen, Cynth . . . Better be going.

(*He crosses the room quickly, and leaves.* CYNTHIA *puts down
the Christmas tree, and follows him, closing the door behind
her.*)

Downstairs. CYNTHIA *goes to the front door and opens it.* MAURICE
has put on his jacket and has collected his case.

CYNTHIA: You'll let me know about the barbecue, then, will
you, sweet'eart?

MAURICE: Yeah, course I will. Tell 'er if she can't make it, I'll
give 'er a clump.

CYNTHIA: Not before I do!

MAURICE: Hang on. (*He puts down his case, and gets out his
wallet.*) Shall I say hello to Monica for you?

CYNTHIA: If you like . . . sweet'eart.

(MAURICE *gives her some money.*)

MAURICE: There you go.

CYNTHIA: Thanks, darlin'!

(MAURICE *puts away his wallet, and pats her on the arm.*)

MAURICE: See yer.
CYNTHIA: (*Affecting lightness*) Ta-ta!
    (MAURICE *leaves.* CYNTHIA *closes the door behind him.*)

*A little later. An empty Victorian pub. Under the huge antique
portrait of a forgotten dignitary,* MAURICE *sits, alone, with a pint of
lager.*

Later still, he sits with MONICA *at their kitchen table. They drink
coffee. Rich, late afternoon light.*
MAURICE: What was your mum like when your dad died?
MONICA: What d'you mean?
MAURICE: How'd she cope?
MONICA: I dunno . . . too young to remember. She just got on
    with it, I suppose, like everyone else.
MAURICE: Did you have to look after Craig?
MONICA: What, you mean like your big sister looked after you?
    No, I did not.
MAURICE: My dad never said a word about my mum after she'd
    died.
MONICA: That's men for you.
MAURICE: I hated him for it. He must've been in real pain.

Maybe he just couldn't share it. (*Pause.*) I didn't know
what I felt. (*Pause.*) I still don't.

MONICA: Cynthia's antics couldn't have helped him much.

MAURICE: D'you miss Craig?

MONICA: How would I miss Craig?

MAURICE: Well, he's your brother.

MONICA: He's in Saudi Arabia, isn' 'e?

MAURICE: Yeah.

MONICA: Well . . . I don't exactly miss 'im. Why? D'you miss
Cynthia? (*Pause.*) D'you think Roxanne's serious about
this scaffolder bloke?

MAURICE: Well, she's only known him for five minutes.

MONICA: Mind you, I was married at her age, wasn't I?
(MAURICE *chuckles slightly.*)
I wonder if she knows.

MAURICE: What, about us?

MONICA: What's there to know about us?

MAURICE: You know what I mean.

MONICA: How would she know about that? Unless you've told
her?

MAURICE: I haven't told her!

MONICA: I hope Cynthia doesn't know, either.

MAURICE: She doesn't.
(*Pause.*)

MONICA: No, I meant . . . if she knows . . . about Cynthia –
you know, before she was born.

MAURICE: I don't know . . . I don't know.

MONICA: I mean, she's got a half-brother or a half-sister
knockin' about somewhere – she's got a right to know.

MAURICE: That's up to Cynthia. You'd never say anything,
would you?

MONICA: Of course not.

MAURICE: Good. Anyway, she must've told her.

MONICA: She never told her who her father was.

MAURICE: None of us knew who he was. I wonder if she ever
misses him.

MONICA: Who?

MAURICE: Roxanne.

MONICA: You can't miss what you never had.

MAURICE: Can't you? (*Pause. He chuckles sadly.*) I was gonna
    kill 'im. Poor Cynthia.
MONICA: Saint Cynthia!
MAURICE: She tried her best.
MONICA: Did she?
MAURICE: Yeah. Yeah, she did. She gave me a lot of love.
    (*Overcome, he gets up and goes to the end of the garden.*
    MONICA *watches him. Tears appear in her eyes.*)

CYNTHIA*'s house. The hall.* ROXANNE, *followed by* CYNTHIA,
comes out of the living-room. She puts on her coat.
CYNTHIA: What shall I tell 'im if 'e phones, then?
ROXANNE: 'Oo?
CYNTHIA: Maurice.
ROXANNE: I don't know – tell 'im what you want.
CYNTHIA: Are you going to bring your bloke or not?
ROXANNE: No, I ain't!
CYNTHIA: 'Ave you asked 'im?
ROXANNE: No!!
    (*The phone rings. She picks it up.*)
    'Ello?
CYNTHIA: That'll be 'im now.
ROXANNE: 'Ello?
CYNTHIA: Let me talk to 'im.
ROXANNE: Shut it! (*She listens.*) There ain't no one there. (*She
    opens the door, and goes out.*)
CYNTHIA: Sweet'eart!
ROXANNE: Will you stop going on about this fuckin' barbecue?
    (CYNTHIA *follows her out on to the pavement.*)
CYNTHIA: You're going to see 'im now, in't you, you can ask
    him.
ROXANNE: I don't even know if I want 'im to go, an' it ain't for
    ages, anyway! See yer later.
    (CYNTHIA *watches her go.*)

Inside a C of E church. A marriage ceremony is taking place.
VICAR: I, Zoë,
BRIDE: I, Zoë . . .
VICAR: Take you, Darren,

BRIDE: Take you, Darren . . .
VICAR: To be my husband.
> (*And so on.* MAURICE *sits alone, at the back of the congregation.*)

At the same moment, MONICA *also sits alone, on her stairs.*

Back at the church, the wedding continues. MAURICE *gets up discreetly, and sets up his camera in the aisle.*
VICAR: Darren and Zoë have given their consent, and made their marriage vows to each other. They have declared their marriage by the joining of hands, and by the giving and receiving of rings; I therefore proclaim that they are Husband and Wife!
> (MAURICE *snaps once.*)

Another summer's evening. CYNTHIA *and* ROXANNE *relax in their back garden.* CYNTHIA *lies on a plastic sunbed.* ROXANNE *sits in a chair, reading the newspaper.*
CYNTHIA: Ain't you seein' 'im tonight, then?
ROXANNE: I'm 'avin' an early night.
CYNTHIA: Keep me company.
ROXANNE: I've got a 'angover.

CYNTHIA: You should stop in more often. You are lookin' after yourself with 'im, ain't you, sweet'eart?

ROXANNE: What d'you mean?

CYNTHIA: You know, taking care. I don't want to ask you nothin' personal darlin', but . . . you takin' the Pill?

ROXANNE: That is personal.

(*Pause.*)

CYNTHIA: Why don't you bring 'im round?

ROXANNE: Leave it out.

CYNTHIA: I'd like to meet 'im – I wouldn't know 'im if 'e stood up in me soup.

ROXANNE: Don't 'old yer breath.

CYNTHIA: You don't wanna leave it up to 'im, darlin' – men are all the same.

ROXANNE: Mum!

CYNTHIA: I 'ope 'e uses a wassername . . . condoms.

ROXANNE: Mind your own business!

CYNTHIA: They can leak. You wanna be careful!

ROXANNE: You're jealous, in't yer?

CYNTHIA: Where is 'e tonight, anyway?

ROXANNE: I dunno.

CYNTHIA: Most likely out givin' somebody else one. That's 'ow I got caught with you . . . runnin' out o' the Pill. You could 'ave a coil fitted.

ROXANNE: Change your record.

CYNTHIA: Dr Mulholland; make an appointment. You'd suit the sponge.

ROXANNE: Keep your voice down!

CYNTHIA: I got a Dutch cap floatin' around somewhere upstairs – you could 'ave that . . . run it under the tap, bit of talcum powder – where're you goin'?

(ROXANNE *has got up and rushed into the house.*)

ROXANNE: (*As she goes*) I don't 'ave to listen to this!

CYNTHIA: (*Getting up*) Sweet'eart!!

(*She also rushes into the house.* ROXANNE *dives into her bedroom, slams the door, and sits in a chair.* CYNTHIA *comes down the hall.*)

Roxanne! (*She enters* ROXANNE'S *room.*) Sweet'eart, darlin' – I'm only tryin' to 'elp yer!

44

ROXANNE: Leave me alone!

CYNTHIA: I'm yer mother! (*She sits on* ROXANNE*'s bed.*)

ROXANNE: Get out of my room!

CYNTHIA: It don't matter if you 'ave a little baby, I'll look after it!

ROXANNE: I ain't gettin' pregnant!

CYNTHIA: I'll give up my job.

ROXANNE: It's nothing to do with you!

CYNTHIA: Yes, it bloody is! I'm not 'avin' you droppin' it at my door!!

ROXANNE: (*Getting up*) JESUS CHRIST!

CYNTHIA: (*Getting up*) I'm sorry, darlin', I don't mean –
(*She grabs hold of* ROXANNE, *who pushes her off with some force.*)

ROXANNE: GET OFF!
(CYNTHIA *falls on the bed.* ROXANNE *is in the hall.*)
You make me sick, you stupid bitch!!
(*She rushes out of the front door, slamming it behind her.*
CYNTHIA *lies on the bed, face down, sobbing.*)

ROXANNE *arrives at* PAUL*'s flat, which is in a large, old Victorian house. She rushes up the steps and rings the bell.*

Inside, she and PAUL *tear off their clothes, and embrace enthusiastically.*

And at the same moment, HORTENSE, *in her flat, sits with her address book again, still pondering. Suddenly, she picks up the phone and dials.*

The phone rings as CYNTHIA *half-sits, half-lies, awkwardly, on* ROXANNE*'s bed, tears streaming down her face. She staggers to the phone in the hall, and lifts the receiver.*

CYNTHIA: Hello?

HORTENSE: I'm sorry to trouble you, but I'm trying to locate a Cynthia Purley.

CYNTHIA: Yes?

HORTENSE: Is that Cynthia Purley?

CYNTHIA: Yes.

HORTENSE: Cynthia Rose Purley?
CYNTHIA: Yes!
HORTENSE: Of 76 Quilter Street?
CYNTHIA: Yes – what is it you want, darlin'?
    (HORTENSE *doesn't say anything.*)
    Hello? Did you want Roxanne? She's gone out.
HORTENSE: No . . .
CYNTHIA: She ain't in any trouble, is she?
HORTENSE: No, it's about Elizabeth.
CYNTHIA: Elizabeth? Elizabeth 'oo?
HORTENSE: Elizabeth Purley.
CYNTHIA: Oh . . . oh, but she's dead.
HORTENSE: No, she isn't.
CYNTHIA: She is, darlin' – I should know.
HORTENSE: I should know.
CYNTHIA: Look, sweet'eart, she's me mother – she went in
    1961.
HORTENSE: No, I mean Baby Elizabeth Purley.
CYNTHIA: Baby Eliz . . .? 'Oo is this?
HORTENSE: She was born on the twenty-third of July, 1968, at
    . . . sorry about this . . . (*She rummages through the
    documents which are on the floor, and finds one.*) Er, yeah, at
    The Haven, Wells Grange Avenue, Sutton, Surrey.

46

(CYNTHIA *is horrified and terrified.*)

HORTENSE: Look, I'm sorry, I know this must be a shock to you –

(CYNTHIA *hangs up abruptly, and rushes out to the scullery, where she vomits into the sink.*)

HORTENSE *puts down the receiver, gets up, and goes towards the door of her living-room. She hesitates for a moment, and looks back at the phone. Then she goes out of the room. After a few moments, she returns, goes straight to the phone, sits down, picks it up, and presses the 'repeat' button.*

The phone rings as CYNTHIA *is washing her face, still at the scullery sink. She turns in horror. She picks up a tea-towel and half-wipes her face and hands. She hesitates for a while. Then she moves slowly towards the phone on the hall stand. She picks up the receiver.*

CYNTHIA: Listen, darlin', what is it you want?

HORTENSE: Look, I'm really sorry . . .

CYNTHIA: You mustn't come round 'ere, sweet'eart.

(*Pause.*)

HORTENSE: I didn't wanna upset you.

CYNTHIA: You mustn't do that. And you mustn't phone, neither.

HORTENSE: I just needed to know.

CYNTHIA: (*Crying*) Yes, but you can't come round 'ere, 'cos no one knows about you, see?

HORTENSE: Right.

CYNTHIA: Promise me you won't come round – promise me!

HORTENSE: Look. (*Sighing.*) I've got your address – if I'd wanted to come round, I'd 'ave done it already.

CYNTHIA: I'm ever so sorry, sweet'eart. (*Her crying is getting worse.*) I'm a little bit upset. Promise me you won't come round.

HORTENSE: All right, I promise.

CYNTHIA: Thank you. Thank you.

(*Pause.*)

HORTENSE: Em . . . Can I meet you, somewhere?

CYNTHIA: Oh, I shouldn't think so, darlin'.

HORTENSE: See, I've got lots of, em . . . I've got lots of questions I want to ask you.

47

CYNTHIA: Yeah, well – I've gotta go now . . .
HORTENSE: Please.
 (*Long pause.*)
CYNTHIA: What's your name, anyway? Eh?
HORTENSE: Hortense.
CYNTHIA: Hortense?
HORTENSE: Yeah.
CYNTHIA: Hortense what?
HORTENSE: Cumberbatch.
CYNTHIA: Clumberbunch? That's a funny name, isn't it?
HORTENSE: Yeah, I suppose it is.
CYNTHIA: You on the phone?
HORTENSE: Yeah – d'you wanna take my number down?
CYNTHIA: Oh, I don't think I've got a pencil.
HORTENSE: I'll wait.
 (CYNTHIA *lowers the receiver, but doesn't move. Her crying gets*
 worse. She raises her hand to her face, and reveals that she is
 holding a ballpoint pen. She puts the receiver to her ear.)
CYNTHIA: I got one.
HORTENSE: (*Overcome*) Er, it's 0171–219 . . . sorry, 619 . . . 4840.
CYNTHIA: Yeah – ta-ra. (*She hangs up.*)

HORTENSE *is left suspended. Then she puts down the receiver. She is*
slightly exasperated.

CYNTHIA *tears* HORTENSE*'s phone number off the newspaper she's*
written it on.

Night. CYNTHIA *is sitting at the bottom of the stairs, nursing the bit*
of paper, and smoking a cigarette. She is no longer crying. She
unfolds the bit of paper, and looks at it anxiously.

HORTENSE*'s bathroom. She is running the bath. She is wearing a*
bath-towel and a headscarf. The phone rings. She turns off the
tap. As she turns round, we see that her face is covered with a
white mud-pack. She rushes to the living-room, and picks up the
receiver.
HORTENSE: Hello.
 (*There is no reply.*)

Hello?

CYNTHIA: D'you wanna meet me or not, then?

HORTENSE: Oh, hello!

CYNTHIA: Yes or no – it's up to you.

HORTENSE: Yeah – 'course I wanna meet you!

CYNTHIA: Well, then . . .

HORTENSE: Are you sure about this? I mean, if you're not
sure . . .

CYNTHIA: Where d'you wanna meet me?

HORTENSE: Well, where would you like to meet?

CYNTHIA: I don't know anywhere . . . Not here, though!!

HORTENSE: No, of course not. Er . . . what about outside
Holborn Tube Station?

CYNTHIA: (*Writing*) 'Olborn . . . When?

HORTENSE: What are you doing this Saturday coming?

CYNTHIA: Nothing – I'm never bloody doing anything.

HORTENSE: Saturday, then.

CYNTHIA: What time?

HORTENSE: Seven-thirty?

CYNTHIA: 'Alf-past seven . . . Now listen: you mustn't phone
me 'ere again, d'you understand me? Otherwise I won't
come and meet yer! Now I'll see you on Sat'day. (*She
hangs up.*)

HORTENSE: Hello . . . (*To receiver*) Don't even know what you look like! (*She sighs and hangs up.*)

Daytime. CYNTHIA *comes through her front door with the shopping.* ROXANNE *is just coming down the stairs, wearing a towel on her head, and an old dressing-gown.*

CYNTHIA: Hello, sweet'eart.

ROXANNE: What's for tea?

CYNTHIA: Got you a bit o' steak.

ROXANNE: What for?

CYNTHIA: Little treat for yer.

ROXANNE: Ain't you 'avin' none?

CYNTHIA: Oh, I'll just fry meself an egg – d'you wanna beer?

ROXANNE: We ain't got none.

CYNTHIA: I got you some.

ROXANNE: Oh. Did yer? (*She goes into the living-room.*)

CYNTHIA: You goin' out?

ROXANNE: No, I'm stayin' in.

    (CYNTHIA *goes into the kitchen, puts down the shopping, and takes off her coat.*)

CYNTHIA: I'm gonna 'ave a few early nights. I've decided.

Holborn Underground Station. Daylight on a summer's evening.

Plenty of people and traffic around. HORTENSE *stands waiting outside the station. After a while, she moves along the pavement. She walks right past* CYNTHIA, *who is standing by the entrance, smoking. Neither notices the other.* HORTENSE *stops for a moment, then returns, passing* CYNTHIA *again. Still neither notices the other.* HORTENSE *comes back a third time. She stops, and looks in* CYNTHIA's *direction. An elderly lady, wearing glasses and carrying a suitcase, emerges from inside the station, and comes to a halt for a moment between* HORTENSE *and* CYNTHIA. HORTENSE *walks towards this lady, but passes her, and goes to* CYNTHIA. *The lady walks away.*

HORTENSE: 'Scuse me.

CYNTHIA: What is it, sweet'eart?

HORTENSE: Are you Cynthia?

CYNTHIA: (*Surprised*) Yeah – 'ow d'you know?

HORTENSE: Hello – I'm Hortense.

    (*She holds out her hand.* CYNTHIA *doesn't take it.*)

CYNTHIA: What're you talkin' about?

HORTENSE: Hortense Cumberbatch – I spoke to you on the
    telephone . . .?

CYNTHIA: What, that was you?

HORTENSE: Yeah.

CYNTHIA: Oh, no – no, sweet'eart – no, darlin' . . . you've been
    ringin' the wrong person.

HORTENSE: Cynthia Purley.

CYNTHIA: Where d'you get my name from, anyway?

HORTENSE: It's on my Birth Certificate. (*She takes the large
    envelope out of her bag.*)

CYNTHIA: What're you talkin' about, 'me Birth Certificate'? It
    can't be.

HORTENSE: It's got your name and your address on it. (*She
    shows the Birth Certificate to* CYNTHIA.) There.

CYNTHIA: No, that's all wrong, darlin' – they've made a mistake
    down the offices. You wanna get down there – get that
    sorted. That's someone 'avin' a joke.

    (HORTENSE *puts the Birth Certificate away.*)

HORTENSE: I don't think so.

CYNTHIA: Let me 'ave a look at that.

    (HORTENSE *gives it to her. She unfolds it, looks at it, and gives*

it back to HORTENSE.) I'm ever so sorry, sweet'eart. I must
be a bit of a disappointment for you. (*She has begun to cry.
She turns away.*)
HORTENSE: Look, I really think you ought to see these
documents.
CYNTHIA: Why, what is it?
HORTENSE: Why don't we, er . . . go . . . somewhere and have
– and sit down?
CYNTHIA: No, I think I'd better be goin', darlin'.
HORTENSE: Here, look, you've come all this way – please! Let's
– let's go and have a cup of tea, or something. There's
places down there.
(CYNTHIA *makes a gesture of agreement.*)
Come on.
(*They set off.*)

An empty café. CYNTHIA *and* HORTENSE *sit side by side at a table.
Each has a cup and saucer.* HORTENSE *is getting out the documents.*
CYNTHIA: I 'ope you find yer mum, sweet'eart. You keep
lookin'. Go on. (*Offers* HORTENSE *a cigarette.*)
HORTENSE: No thanks. I don't smoke.
CYNTHIA: (*Lighting up*) Nor should yer. My daughter smokes
like a chimney.
HORTENSE: You got a daughter?
CYNTHIA: Yeah. I ain't never been in 'ere before. They
shouldn't go raisin' yer 'opes like that – it ain't fair!
(HORTENSE *puts a document on the table.*)
HORTENSE: Is this your signature?
(CYNTHIA *looks at it. Then she picks it up.*)
CYNTHIA: This is stupid – I don't understand it. I mean, I can't
be your mother, can I?
HORTENSE: Why not?
CYNTHIA: Well, look at me.
HORTENSE: What?
CYNTHIA: Listen, I don't mean nothin' by it, darlin', but I ain't
never been with a black man in my life. No disrespect, nor
nothing. I'd a' remembered, wouldn't I?
(HORTENSE *looks at* CYNTHIA. CYNTHIA *thinks about things.
Long pause. Suddenly, something comes back to her.*)

Oh, bloody 'ell . . .! (*She looks at* HORTENSE.) Oh, Jesus
Christ Almighty! (*She bursts into uncontrollable tears, and
turns away from* HORTENSE.) I'm sorry, sweet'eart . . .
(*Sobbing.*) I'm so ashamed.

HORTENSE: You shouldn't be ashamed. (*She puts away the
documents.*)

CYNTHIA: I can't look at you. (*She turns to* HORTENSE.) I didn't
know, sweet'eart, honest, I didn't know.

HORTENSE: What didn't you know?

CYNTHIA: I didn't know you was black. See, I th – I thought
they got the dates all wrong; all this time I thought you was
born six – six weeks premature, but you wasn't . . . you
wasn't . . .
(*Pause.*)

HORTENSE: Who was 'e?

CYNTHIA: You don't wanna know that, darlin'.

HORTENSE: I do.

CYNTHIA: Listen, I wanna be honest with you, but I can't tell
you that, sweet'eart, I'm sorry. (*Pause.*) I'm sorry. Look at
yer. 'Spect I'm a bit of a disappointment to you, ain' I?

HORTENSE: No.

CYNTHIA: You don' 'ave to say that, darlin'.

HORTENSE: I know.

53

CYNTHIA: You've been better off without me, I'll tell you that much. I done you a good turn.

HORTENSE: Your tea's getting cold.

(CYNTHIA *sips her tea.*)

CYNTHIA: What's your mum like, then? Does she mind you lookin' for me?

HORTENSE: My mum died recently.

CYNTHIA: Oh – I'm sorry. What about yer dad?

HORTENSE: He's dead, an' all.

(CYNTHIA *cries quietly.*)

Are you married?

CYNTHIA: No, no . . . em, I ain't . . . I ain't married, sweet'eart. (*Pause.*) Are you?

HORTENSE: No.

CYNTHIA: I bet you got a boyfriend, though, ain't yer?

HORTENSE: No, not at the moment.

CYNTHIA: Nice-lookin' girl like you?

(*Pause.*)

HORTENSE: Have you got a boyfriend?

CYNTHIA: Oh, I give 'em all a wide berth; they got me into enough trouble in the past, ain't they? (*She laughs, a little hysterically. She continues laughing. Gradually, this laugh turns into a cry. Then she wipes an eye.*) You got a job, 'ave yer?

HORTENSE: Yeah.

CYNTHIA: That's good. What doin'?

HORTENSE: I'm an optometrist.

CYNTHIA: Eh?

HORTENSE: I test eyes. Optician?

CYNTHIA: Are you? Well . . . there's a turn-up.

HORTENSE: What do you do?

CYNTHIA: I work in a factory.

HORTENSE: D'you like it?

CYNTHIA: It pays the rent.

HORTENSE: How about your daughter?

CYNTHIA: She works for the council. You got any sisters?

HORTENSE: No, two brothers.

CYNTHIA: Are they, um . . . adopted?

HORTENSE: No.

CYNTHIA: What d'they do?

54

HORTENSE: One's a computer salesman, and the other one's got his own garage.

CYNTHIA: I bet your mum was proud o' you, wasn't she?

HORTENSE: Yes, she was.

CYNTHIA: Yeah, course she was! I'd've been proud!
(*Pause.*)

HORTENSE: Why didn't you wanna see me?

CYNTHIA: Well, 'cos nobody knows about you, sweet'eart. I don't want to upset my daughter, do I?

HORTENSE: I mean, when I was born.

CYNTHIA: Well, I couldn't . . . I was too upset, see – they wanted me to look at you . . . they wanted me to 'old you, but I couldn't, I just couldn't. (*She starts crying again.*) I didn't know if I was comin' or goin' – I was only a little girl meself, sixteen. I didn't 'ave no choice. If I 'ad o' seen yer, I'd 'ave wanted to keep yer – you do believe me, don't yer, sweet'eart? (*Pause.*) I don't blame you, darlin'. You only just found out?

HORTENSE: No. I've known since I was seven.

CYNTHIA: What, your mum and dad told you, did they?

HORTENSE: Yeah, they did.

CYNTHIA: They sound like nice people.

HORTENSE: Yeah. My mum told me on the plane on our way back from Barbados.

CYNTHIA: Little girl . . . was yer upset?

HORTENSE: I just looked out at the clouds.
(*They both reflect for a moment.*)

In HORTENSE's *car.*

HORTENSE: Haven't you ever thought about me?

CYNTHIA: Yeah, of course I 'ave. But 'tain't no good pinin' over what you ain't got, is it?

HORTENSE: But didn't you think I'd look for you?

CYNTHIA: No. I didn't, as it 'appens. Wish you 'adn't bothered now, don't yer?

HORTENSE: No. I'm glad. I don't want to disrupt your family or anything . . . I just had to see you. I had to know who you were.

CYNTHIA: Listen . . . I wanna wish you all the best, sweet'eart,

whatever you do. An' I'll be thinkin' of yer.
(*Tears well in her eyes.* HORTENSE *drives on.*)

Bright evening sun on the corner of CYNTHIA*'s street.* HORTENSE*'s car pulls up, and* CYNTHIA *gets out. She walks a few feet, then turns and waves, and carries on.* HORTENSE *waits a moment, then drives off.*

CYNTHIA *and* ROXANNE *are smoking cigarettes after a meal at their kitchen table.* CYNTHIA *is reading a magazine.*
ROXANNE: Quiet, ain't yer? What's up?
CYNTHIA: (*Looking up*) You goin' out?
ROXANNE: Yeah, in a bit. Feelin' all right?
CYNTHIA: Oh, there's nothing the matter with me, sweet'eart.
    Nothing at all. (*Pause.*) D'you find anything today?
ROXANNE: Frozen chicken.
CYNTHIA: What, in the road?
ROXANNE: No, in a bin. Still cold. Some dirty magazines . . .
CYNTHIA: D'you bring 'em 'ome?
ROXANNE: No!
    (*Pause.*)
CYNTHIA: Still, I suppose there are worse jobs. Gotta laugh,
    ain't yer, sweet'eart? (*Pause.*) Else you'd cry.
    (*They sit smoking.*)

A little later. ROXANNE *leaves the house.*

And not long after that, CYNTHIA, *in her hall, dials a phone number.*

HORTENSE *is sitting on her sofa. She is reading a paperback book* (Wild Swans *by Jung Chang*). *The phone rings beside her. She picks it up.*
HORTENSE: Hello?
CYNTHIA: Is that Hortense?
HORTENSE: Speaking.
CYNTHIA: It's Cynthia.
HORTENSE: Hello.
CYNTHIA: I didn't think you'd be in.

HORTENSE: I am. (*She laughs slightly.*)

CYNTHIA: Well, I just, um . . . wanted to ring up and say . . . 'ow nice it was to meet yer yesterday – that's all.

HORTENSE: Thank you.

CYNTHIA: Been thinkin' about yer all day.

HORTENSE: I've been thinkin' about you.

CYNTHIA: Yeah, well, um . . . I just wanted to say that.

HORTENSE: Thank you.

CYNTHIA: I don't know what to say now – daft, ain' it? (*Pause.*) Got 'ome all right, did you?

HORTENSE: Yeah – thank you! (*Pause.*) What've you been doing today?

CYNTHIA: Oh, just out the back, sunning meself. What you been doin'?

HORTENSE: Just chillin' out, really.

CYNTHIA: Yeah, 'ot, ain' it?

HORTENSE: Yeah.

(*She laughs quietly. Pause.*)

CYNTHIA: Well, that's all I wanted to say, sweet'eart. Ta-ta, then.

HORTENSE: I'd really like to see you again.

CYNTHIA: Would yer?

HORTENSE: Yeah.

CYNTHIA: Oh, that'd be nice.

HORTENSE: D'you like Italian food?

CYNTHIA: Yeah, eat anything, me . . . Chinese, kebabs, the lot!

(HORTENSE *laughs.*)

What?

HORTENSE: Nothing! It's great!

(*They are both smiling.*)

Outside a suburban antique shop, MONICA *is looking at a sale of houseplants. She carries a shopping bag.*

In MAURICE*'s studio, an attractive young woman is posing for her photograph.*

MAURICE: And – (*He snaps.*) Okay . . . other side, please.

(*The* WOMAN *turns towards us to reveal a very severe scar down one side of her face.*)

MAURICE: And – (*He snaps. She blinks nervously in the flashlight.*)

Lovely. So if you'd bring your face round this way.
Please . . .?

WOMAN: Can you shut the door, please?

(MAURICE *looks round towards the door.*)

MAURICE: Yes, sure. (*He goes and closes the door. Just as he does
so,* JANE, *his assistant, is walking past with a plastic watering
can.* MAURICE *comes back to his camera. He looks through the
viewfinder.*) Sorry. So who did your original photographs?

WOMAN: My dad, actually, but my solicitor said that they
weren't good enough.

MAURICE: Did you have a police photographer?

WOMAN: (*Surprised*) No!

(MAURICE *snaps, then moves the camera nearer to her.*)

MAURICE: I'm just going to come in a bit closer, so I hope you
don't suffer from claustrophobia.

WOMAN: No, I don't actually.

MAURICE: That's good. (*He looks through the viewfinder and
focuses the lens.*) Okay, so we're just gonna . . . move –
(*He moves close to her, and goes to adjust her hair, but she
flinches slightly, and adjusts it herself.*)

WOMAN: Thank you!

MAURICE: (*Quietly*) Sorry . . . 'T's great . . .

(*The* WOMAN *recomposes herself.*)

And – (*He snaps.*) A little bit closer. (*He moves the camera
again, and looks through it.*) Now . . . I know this isn't very
nice, but it's gotta be done, hasn't it? (*He moves a floodlamp.*)

WOMAN: I want them to look as bad as possible.

MAURICE: Of course.

WOMAN: I lost my job – I was good at my job!

MAURICE: What did you do?

WOMAN: I'm a beauty consultant.

(MAURICE *looks at her for a moment.*)

MAURICE: Okay, now if you just bring your chin up . . . a little
bit.

(*She does so.*)

Lovely, and – (*He snaps.*) So what actually happened to
you?

(*Pause.*)

WOMAN: My seat-belt was broken – I went through the

windscreen. It wasn't my car, I wasn't drivin' – it wasn't my fault.

MAURICE: Yeah, you said.

WOMAN: It wasn't!

(MAURICE *snaps. She blinks nervously.*)

MAURICE: You okay?

(*Pause.*)

WOMAN: Mm.

(MAURICE *lowers the camera on the tripod.*)

MAURICE: Did the driver sustain any injuries?

WOMAN: No, unfortunately.

MAURICE: He's obviously not in your good books.

WOMAN: I haven't seen 'im since – I don't wanna see 'im, either.

MAURICE: Life isn't fair, is it? Someone always draws the short straw. (*He looks through the camera.*) Okay, that's very good. (*He snaps.*) One more . . .

A few minutes later, in MAURICE's *reception area. The* WOMAN *stands waiting. She is now wearing dark glasses.* JANE *and* MAURICE *both come in, she from the back office, he from the studio.*

JANE: Here's your receipt.

WOMAN: (*Taking it*) Thank you.

MAURICE: Give us a ring in the morning, and we'll see what we can do.

WOMAN: Fine.

(JANE *opens the street door for her, and she goes.*)

JANE: 'Bye, then! Mind 'ow you go!

(*She closes the door. She and* MAURICE *both watch the* WOMAN *as she crosses the road.*)

Oh, Maurice, that's terrible. 'Ow'd she do that, then?

MAURICE: Car crash.

JANE: Oh . . . she's so lovely!

MAURICE: Not any more, she isn't.

JANE: It's tragic.

MAURICE: She's getting some ear-'ole from that dosser, now!

JANE: Oh, he's been lookin' at me – gives me the creeps!

(*And, indeed, as* JANE *and* MAURICE *were talking about the* WOMAN *a few moments ago, we saw a small, shabbily dressed man with longish hair get up from a public bench, and call after her. Now* MAURICE *moves to a different position in order to get a better view of the window.*)

MAURICE: I don't believe it.

(*The* WOMAN *has got into her car, and is now driving off, watched by the 'dosser'.*)

JANE: 'Ow much money d'you think she'd get, then?

MAURICE: What?

JANE: Insurance.

MAURICE: Oh, if she's lucky, fifteen, twenty grand.

JANE: I don't know what I'd do if that happened to me . . think I'd kill meself.

(*She leaves* MAURICE, *who continues to look out of the window. The 'dosser' now seems to be looking back at* MAURICE *from the other side of the road. At this moment,* MONICA *comes into the shop.*)

MAURICE: Hello.

MONICA: Hiya!

MAURICE: I didn't expect to see you.

MONICA: Oh, I'm terribly sorry!

JANE: (*Waving through hatch*) Hello, Monica.

MONICA: Hi, Jane!

(MONICA *and* MAURICE *kiss.*)

Just been for a facial – I'm dyin' for a cuppa tea!

MAURICE: Look over there.

MONICA: What?

MAURICE: That bloke.

MONICA: What bloke?

MAURICE: See who it is?

MONICA: What, by the lamppost?

MAURICE: Yeah. It's Stuart Christian, isn't it?

MONICA: No!

MAURICE: It is.

MONICA: But he's in Sydney.

MAURICE: Is he?

MONICA: He's comin' over.

('STUART' *is, indeed, crossing the road.*)

MAURICE: He doesn't look very well, does he?

JANE: 'Ere's that man!

MAURICE: 'T's all right, Jane, we know 'im.

60

JANE: Do yer?

MONICA: What's he want?

MAURICE: God knows.

MONICA: Well, it's over to you, then, Buster! (*She joins* JANE *behind the hatch.*)

MAURICE: Thanks very much!

(*As* 'STUART' *enters the shop,* JANE *twists the slats of the Venetian blind to the closed position.*)

MAURICE: Hello, Stuart!

STUART: Maurice!

MAURICE: Long time no see! (*He holds out his hand.*)

STUART: Yeah. (*He takes* MAURICE'*s hand, and shakes it.*) How's things?

MAURICE: Fine, thanks, fine!

STUART: Good . . .

MAURICE: You're looking well.

STUART: You're still here, then?

MAURICE: Yup.

STUART: Good.

(*Pause.*)

MAURICE: I thought we'd lost you to Australia!

STUART: (*Holding up his hands*) Well . . .!! How's the wife and kids? – Maureen.

MAURICE: Monica. I haven't got any kids.

STUART: Haven't you?

MAURICE: No. She's great, thanks.

(STUART *ponders for a moment. He is unaware of* MONICA *and* JANE *peering through the blind.*)

STUART: Good on you, mate!

(MAURICE *laughs slightly.* STUART *crosses the room, and sits down. Pause.*)

MAURICE: You still in the game?

STUART: Look at all this! What're you doing? It's lost its style, Maurice!

MAURICE: Has it?

STUART: Looks like a dentist's waiting-room.

(MAURICE *chuckles.*)

I'd kill for a cuppa tea.

A few minutes later. MAURICE'*s back office, behind the hatch.*
STUART *is sitting at the desk.* MAURICE *and* MONICA *are standing.*
STUART: If you're twenty-one . . . or a millionaire . . . it's great.
Or you've got nine kids . . . you're fine! Brilliant! Open
arms! But for guys like you and me . . . doesn't matter how
good you are . . . forget it. But it was an experience, and
now I'm back.
MONICA: That's too bad! You were full of such big plans, as
well.
STUART: Well, it's a big place.
MONICA: That's true.
STUART: Too fuckin' big. You're lookin' as gorgeous as ever,
Monica! (*He looks* MONICA *up and down.*)
MAURICE: So, Stuart, are you thinkin' about settin' up again?
STUART: No, forget it. Too much of a pain. You know what it's
like, Maurice! You sweat your balls off for years, you try
and make people happy . . . and what d'you get back?
Nothing!
(JANE *gives out mugs of tea.*)
MONICA: Thanks.
(STUART *ignores* JANE*: he is flicking through* MAURICE'*s desk
diary.*)
MAURICE: By the way, Stuart, this is Jane, my assistant. This is
Mr Christian, the gentleman I bought the business from.
JANE: Hello.
STUART: Hiya, Jane! I hope he's treatin' you well.
JANE: He's all right.
STUART: You can work for me any time.
JANE: I'm all right where I am, thank you.
(STUART *has taken out a hip flask; he pours a drop of spirit
into his tea.* MONICA *and* MAURICE *exchange looks.*)
MONICA: Your wife must've been sorry to have come back.
STUART: Which wife? Oh, that bitch! She never came out there
in the first place.
MONICA: Oh?
MAURICE: So where are you living at the moment, Stuart?
STUART: Down at Grays.
MAURICE: Essex?
STUART: Yeah . . . me mother's place.

MAURICE: Must be nice for her.

MONICA: Havin' her boy to fuss over!

STUART: She's dead. She died when I was still in Bangkok.

JANE: (*Sentimental*) Aah!

(MAURICE *is quietly amused by this, in spite of himself.*)

MAURICE: Sorry to hear that.

MONICA: It's a shame.

STUART: Didn't see much of 'er, anyway. It's my dad I miss.
You win some, you lose some.
(*He is overcome. He sips some tea. His hand is shaking, and the mug rattles against his teeth. Pause.*)

MONICA: (*Brightly*) You must have had some lovely weather in Australia!

STUART: Too hot. It's too hot over there; it's too cold over here.
(*He takes a final swig of tea, puts down his cup, gets up, and leaves the room abruptly.* MAURICE *shrugs at* MONICA, *and follows him.* MONICA *and* JANE *move to a better vantage point for watching what happens next.*)

STUART *is in* MAURICE's *studio.* MAURICE *joins him.*

STUART: Hasn't changed much in here.

MAURICE: No, just a lick of paint.

STUART: Still got the Bronica, then?

MAURICE: Yep.

STUART: Should've thought you'd have been able to afford a
Hasselblad by now, Maurice!

MAURICE: I can.

STUART: You're well off, are you?

MAURICE: Hm. Surviving, mate.

STUART: Yeah . . . you've done very well out of my business,
'aven't yer?

MAURICE: My business.

STUART: No, it's my business –

MAURICE: No, Stuart, no: it used to be your business – I
bought it from you, it's my business.

STUART: Listen, this was an antique shop . . .

MAURICE: That's right.

STUART: There was nothing here!

MAURICE: That's right, I know.

STUART: I gave you my goodwill; I gave you my clientele; I gave you my fucking reputation!

MAURICE: You gave me nothing, Stuart. With all due respect, your client-list was shit.

STUART: It wasn't . . .

MAURICE: I followed it up. I wrote to them, I rang 'em; I didn't get one bite. If there's any success in this shop, it's down to me.

STUART: That's bollocks!

MAURICE: No, it's not bollocks, Stuart – it's the truth.

STUART: How many weddings d'you do?

MAURICE: Oh, enough.

STUART: How many?

MAURICE: Oh, about forty a year.

STUART: I used to do a hundred and forty!

MAURICE: What, personally?

STUART: No, not personally, no – nobody does 'em personally!

MAURICE: I do.

STUART: Well, then, you're a bloody fool! You get people in, get 'em out there! If the work's there, take it – you've got to grab it while you can!

MAURICE: It's not in my interest to get some tosser in – I mean, I'll have no control – it could fuck up my reputation!

STUART: I'm not a tosser!

MAURICE: I didn't say you were!

STUART: I'm not a fuckin' tosser!

MAURICE: I'm not talking about you.

STUART: Don't call me a tosser!

MAURICE: I wasn't talkin' about you, Stuart!

STUART: I can still do it. I've still got an eye. They can't teach you that. I'm still a photographer!

MAURICE: Course you are.

(*Pause.*)

STUART: So if you want someone to help you out, no worries, mate. It'll be all right.

MAURICE: Right . . . right, I see what you're saying, Stuart, yeah. I'll bear it in mind.

STUART: Can you lend me a camera?

MAURICE: Yeah, sure.

STUART: I had mine nicked. (*Pause.*) Yeah, great. Thanks . . .
(*He shakes* MAURICE*'s hand.*)
MAURICE: Sure.

Moments later, STUART *leaves the shop.*
MONICA: I thought we were never gonna get rid of 'im.
(MAURICE *is looking in* STUART*'s direction.*)
MAURICE: There but for the grace of God.
(*He turns away, and attends to his camera.* MONICA *comes into the studio, and looks at him. He doesn't look up. She turns, and looks thoughtfully towards the street.*)

CYNTHIA *is in her kitchen. Daylight.*
CYNTHIA: (*Shouting*) Tea's on the table!
(ROXANNE *is in the living-room, watching television: we hear 'The Man Who Broke the Bank at Monte Carlo' being played on a Wurlitzer.*)
ROXANNE: Right.
(*She goes into the kitchen, and sits at the table.* CYNTHIA *is serving* ROXANNE*'s food.*)
Ain't you 'avin' none?
CYNTHIA: No.
ROXANNE: Why not?
(CYNTHIA *proceeds to go upstairs. She replies to* ROXANNE*'s last question in the hall.*)
CYNTHIA: I'm goin' out.
ROXANNE: Where are you goin'?
(CYNTHIA *is on the way upstairs.*)

A little later, ROXANNE *is back on the sofa in the living-room. She is watching a comedy show on television (much mirth).* CYNTHIA *comes downstairs. We see her through the open door. She has got dressed up.*
CYNTHIA: I'm off now, then, sweet'eart.
ROXANNE: Ain't you gonna tell me where?
CYNTHIA: You never tell me where you're goin'.
ROXANNE: You don't ever go nowhere!
CYNTHIA: Well, I'm going somewhere tonight. Ta-ta. (*She goes.*)
ROXANNE: 'Ave fun.

66

CYNTHIA: Don't wait up.
(*The front door slams.* ROXANNE *looks bemused. She returns her attention to the television.*)

That evening. ROXANNE *and* PAUL *are walking down the street. Daylight.*

ROXANNE: She's been acting right funny.

PAUL: Where's she gone?

ROXANNE: Well, fuck knows – she wouldn't tell us. 'E's all right, though, Maurice; 'e's always got plenty of wine in, an' that. We'll get well pissed.

PAUL: Yeah – nice one!
(*They go into a pub.*)

About the same time. An Italian restaurant. Several groups of diners. CYNTHIA *and* HORTENSE *sit facing each other. They are sipping white wine.*

CYNTHIA: I'm a little bit shy of you, to tell you the truth, sweet'eart.

HORTENSE: Me? Oh, you shouldn't be!

CYNTHIA: Look at you, sittin' there. You look like a model.

HORTENSE: (*Laughing*) Do I?

CYNTHIA: I bet you was a pretty little girl, wun't yer?

HORTENSE: Yeah, lovely . . . (*She pulls a funny face, which she proceeds to make even more grotesque, finally squinting.*)

CYNTHIA: Don't do that – you'll stay like it!

(HORTENSE *keeps it up for a moment more, then bursts into laughter.*)

Stop it – don't spoil it.

HORTENSE: I used to drive my mum mad, pulling faces.

CYNTHIA: Did you! I bet she was a laugh, wasn't she?

HORTENSE: No, not really.

CYNTHIA: I thought you said she was a midwife.

HORTENSE: Yes, she was.

CYNTHIA: Oh, I'd like to 'ave been one of them. I love babies. (*Pause.*) I'm sorry, darlin'.

HORTENSE: It's all right. Cheers.

(*They clink glasses.*)

Is that all right for you?

CYNTHIA: Yeah, it's lovely. Wet, innit?

(*They both laugh.*)

Where's this food, then? – I'm ravishin'!

(HORTENSE *laughs.*)

What?

(HORTENSE *gestures that it's nothing, and* CYNTHIA *laughs too.*)

HORTENSE: I've got so many things I wanna ask you, but I can't remember what they are.

CYNTHIA: Nice to 'ave somebody to talk to, innit? Give us yer 'and 'ere.

(HORTENSE *gives* CYNTHIA *her hand.* CYNTHIA *strokes her arm.*)

God, you've got beautiful skin!

(HORTENSE *laughs, and looks round.*)

Right, let's 'ave a look at you . . . (*She strokes* HORTENSE*'s palm.*)

HORTENSE: What, can you read palms?

CYNTHIA: I used to. Ain't done it for years – nobody's interested no more. Now, if I didn't know you, I could see just by lookin' 'ere what a nice girl you are. Big 'eart.

(HORTENSE *laughs.*)

Oh, you're gonna live to a ripe old age, an' all. Let's 'ave a look . . . Coupla kids.

HORTENSE: Wow!

CYNTHIA: D'you want babies?

HORTENSE: I'm not sure, really.

CYNTHIA: Oh, don't yer?

HORTENSE: Maybe – I don't know yet.

CYNTHIA: Yeah – course you do! What star sign are you?

HORTENSE: Leo – I'm on the cusp of Cancer.

CYNTHIA: When's your birthday? Oh! 'T's the twenty-third of
July, ain't it? You'd think I'd know that, wouldn't yer?
(*Pause.*) That was the other day, wasn't it?

HORTENSE: Yeah – Sunday.

CYNTHIA: Well, why didn't you say nothin' when I phoned yer?

HORTENSE: 'T's not a big deal.

CYNTHIA: D'you 'ave a party?

HORTENSE: No.

CYNTHIA: What'd you do, then?

HORTENSE: Stayed in; read me book; 'ad a little drink . . .

CYNTHIA: What, on your own?

HORTENSE: Yeah.

CYNTHIA: Aah. Well, 'appy birthday for Sunday, sweet'eart.

HORTENSE: Thank you!

CYNTHIA: You're out now, ain't yer?

HORTENSE: Yeah. In good company.

CYNTHIA: With yer mum!
(HORTENSE *smiles. The waitress brings their food.* HORTENSE *puts on her table-napkin, and they start the meal.*)

Early evening, another day. CYNTHIA *and* ROXANNE *are at their kitchen table.* CYNTHIA *is still eating.* ROXANNE *is smoking a cigarette.*
CYNTHIA: You thought about 'avin' some drivin' lessons?
ROXANNE: What for?
CYNTHIA: I could get yer some for yer birthday.
ROXANNE: Be stupid
CYNTHIA: Get yerself a little motor. Eh?
ROXANNE: Ain't yer goin' out tonight?
CYNTHIA: No.
ROXANNE: Why, what's 'appened?
CYNTHIA: You goin' out?
ROXANNE: Yeah, later.
CYNTHIA: Where you goin'?
ROXANNE: Down the pub – I 'ope you're takin' care o' yourself!
CYNTHIA: What d'you mean?
ROXANNE: You don't want to go getting knocked up, do yer?
CYNTHIA: Don't be so bloody cheeky!
ROXANNE: Not at your age.

Some days later. CYNTHIA *comes out of a hairdressing salon, a scarf on her head. She scuttles across a zebra crossing, and runs into* ROXANNE, *who is at work sweeping the pavement.*
ROXANNE: All right?
CYNTHIA: (*Pointing*) Missed a bit, darlin'!
    (ROXANNE *watches her go.*)

Night. The Odeon cinema. Hundreds of people around. CYNTHIA *and* HORTENSE *emerge from inside. They are having a jolly time.* HORTENSE *helps* CYNTHIA *on with her coat. They link arms and disappear into the crowds.*

In a bar, they are sitting together at a table. They are laughing.
HORTENSE: Who's this? (*She pulls another funny face.*)
CYNTHIA: Oh, don't start all that again!
HORTENSE: Come on, 'oo is it?
CYNTHIA: 'T'ain't me, is it?
HORTENSE: No!
CYNTHIA: Who?
HORTENSE: Sylvester Stallone.
CYNTHIA: I can't understand a word 'e says.
HORTENSE: You like looking' at 'im, though.
CYNTHIA: No, 'e ain't my sort!

HORTENSE: What is your type?

CYNTHIA: What? Film star?

HORTENSE: Yeah.

CYNTHIA: Marlon . . .

(HORTENSE *laughs*.)

I like a bloke with a bit o' meat on 'im. What sort o' bloke d'you go in for, then?

HORTENSE: Um . . . Intelligent . . . Sensitive . . .

CYNTHIA: What, don't you care what they look like?

HORTENSE: Yeah, but they gotta have something goin' on upstairs.

CYNTHIA: You only 'ave black boyfriends, do yer?

HORTENSE: No.

(*They laugh. Pause.*)

CYNTHIA: How d'you look after yourself, then? You know, if you don't wanna 'ave babies?

(*They laugh.*)

HORTENSE: Condoms.

CYNTHIA: Oh, you just stop at that then, do yer?

HORTENSE: Yeah.

CYNTHIA: (*Overlapping*) Yeah, you can't be too careful, can you . . .? These days . . .

HORTENSE: (*Overlapping*) 'T's the best way, really – gotta protect yourself . . .

(*Pause.*)

CYNTHIA: It's my daughter's birthday next week.

HORTENSE: How old is she?

CYNTHIA: Twenty-one.

HORTENSE: Nice age.

CYNTHIA: Well, she's yer sister now, really, ain't she?

HORTENSE: Yeah; suppose she is . . . (*Pause.*) Does she look like you?

CYNTHIA: Yeah, a bit. You look more like me than she does. Same build.

HORTENSE: What are 'er eyes like?

CYNTHIA: Blue. My brother's doin' a party for 'er.

HORTENSE: That's nice – at least it takes the strain off of you.

CYNTHIA: Yeah, well, there is that. Shame you ain't comin', really . . .

HORTENSE: Ah!

CYNTHIA: Meet yer new family. Oh – sweet'eart! I nearly forgot! (*She takes a small wrapped gift out of her bag, and gives it to* HORTENSE.) Happy birthday for Sunday.

HORTENSE: Oh, you shouldn't 'ave bothered.

CYNTHIA: Oh, 't'ain't nothing much!

HORTENSE: Ah! (*She opens it. It's a bottle of bath oil.*) Ah, thank you! (*She kisses* CYNTHIA *on the cheek.*) Don't start crying.

CYNTHIA: Perhaps I should ask him.

HORTENSE: What?

CYNTHIA: If I can take someone.

HORTENSE: Oh, I don't know. It's a family thing, isn't it?

CYNTHIA: Well, you are family, ain't yer? I'm proud of you!

CYNTHIA *is talking on a pay-phone in a booth at her factory. Behind her, through a window, we can see women at work.*

CYNTHIA: Listen, Maurice, sweet'eart . . . I wanted to ask you a favour.

MAURICE: (*Off*) Oh, yeah – what's that, then?

CYNTHIA: You know the party, Sunday?

MAURICE: Barbecue, yeah . . .

CYNTHIA: Yeah. Can I bring a mate? Sweet'eart? (*Pause.*) Hello?

(MAURICE *is standing in his office.* JANE *is in the background, eating crisps.*)

MAURICE: Is it a bloke?

CYNTHIA: Course is ain't a bloke, you silly bugger! Chance'd be a fine thing!

MAURICE: (*Laughing*) Who is it, then?

CYNTHIA: Oh, just someone at work . . . we've been out a couple o' times . . . and I was meant to 'ave seen 'er Sunday, only I forgot. That all right, then?

MAURICE: I suppose so.

CYNTHIA: What d'you mean, you suppose so?

MAURICE: No, it'll be fine.

CYNTHIA: Smashin' . . .

MAURICE: I'll 'ave to check it out, though.

CYNTHIA: Check it out – 'oo with?

MAURICE: Listen – er, if I don't phone you back, bring 'er, all right?

CYNTHIA: I don't want to upset nobody.

MAURICE: No, don't worry.

CYNTHIA: Are you sure, then?

MAURICE: Yeah, yeah – no problem. Yeah.

CYNTHIA: Okay, then, sweet'eart – lookin' forward to it!

MAURICE: All right, yeah, well, say 'ello to Roxanne for me.

CYNTHIA: Yeah. Ta-ra, then.

MAURICE: All right – ta-ra – 'bye, Cynth.

(CYNTHIA *hangs up.*)

CYNTHIA *is on the phone in her hall at home. Daylight.*

CYNTHIA: Listen, I spoke to my little brother today, an' 'e says it's all right, so . . . d'you wanna come, then?

(HORTENSE *is sitting on her bed, a hairbrush in one hand, the phone in the other.*)

HORTENSE: Oh, I dunno . . .

CYNTHIA: I told 'im you was me mate!

HORTENSE: I'd still feel a bit awkward.

CYNTHIA: Oh, don't be daft, sweet'eart – you'll be with me, won't yer?

HORTENSE: It wouldn't feel right.

CYNTHIA: I thought you wanted to come.

HORTENSE: Yeah . . .

CYNTHIA: Oh, well, o' course . . . if you've changed yer mind . . . ?

(HORTENSE *pulls a face.*)

I was looking forward to it.

HORTENSE: Oh, I know . . .

CYNTHIA: What d'yer think, then?

HORTENSE: (*Pulling a face*) All right – I'll come!

CYNTHIA: You comin'?

MAURICE: Yeah.

CYNTHIA: Oh, right, then, sweet'eart – listen: I'll give you a ring, later in the week, and give you the address an' everything . . .

MAURICE: Okay, then.

CYNTHIA: Okay – ta-ta, then.

HORTENSE: Bye-bye!

(CYNTHIA *rings off.* HORTENSE *shakes her head, and pulls a face.*)
Jesus!

MAURICE *and* MONICA*'s bedroom. Daylight.* MONICA *is lying on top of the bed.* MAURICE *is sitting on the side of the bed, next to her, folding up his tie.*
MONICA: You should've just said yes. Makin' me look like a . . . oh . . . I can hardly say no now.
MAURICE: It's up to you.
MONICA: We don't know anything about this person, whoever she is.
MAURICE: It's some new mate – they've been out a few times.
MONICA: Two hysterical nutters!
MAURICE: I'm just glad she's got a friend.
MONICA: Well, I'm going to have a great time!
MAURICE: I thought I'd ask Jane, as well.
MONICA: Anybody else you want to invite? We've only got four garden chairs!
(MAURICE *chuckles.*)
Oh, give us two of them painkillers.
(*She picks up a glass of orange juice.* MAURICE *gives her two pills. She takes these with the juice.*)
MAURICE: D'you fancy some fish and chips?
MONICA: Don't be sarcastic.
MAURICE: I wasn't.

The day of the barbecue. On MONICA *and* MAURICE*'s patio. The table and seven chairs.* MONICA *adds some finishing touches.*

Meanwhile, HORTENSE *stands at her living-room window, looking at the wind in the trees, and contemplating her fate.*

A minicab pulls up at MAURICE *and* MONICA*'s house.* CYNTHIA, ROXANNE *and* PAUL *get out.* CYNTHIA *is carrying a bunch of flowers,* ROXANNE *a bottle of sparkling wine, and* PAUL *a lager four-pack.* ROXANNE *goes straight to the front door, and knocks.* PAUL *pays the driver, and the car leaves.* CYNTHIA *and* PAUL *arrive at the door.*

CYNTHIA: There's a bell 'ere.

ROXANNE: Don't do that, I've just done the knocker!

CYNTHIA: All right!!

(MONICA *opens the door.*)

MONICA: Hello, there!

CYNTHIA: Hallo, sweet'eart! (*She goes straight in.*)

MONICA: You got here in one piece, then?

CYNTHIA: Long time no see!

(*She kisses* MONICA, *and gives her the flowers.* MONICA *is less than enthusiastic about the kiss.*)

MONICA: Yes, that's right – thank you. Hello, Birthday Girl!

(*She hugs and kisses* ROXANNE *very enthusiastically.*)

ROXANNE: (*Smiling*) All right, Monica?

MONICA: Oh, look at you!

ROXANNE: This is Paul.

MONICA: Hello, Paul.

PAUL: How d'you do? (*He shakes hands with* MONICA.)

MONICA: Nice to meet you.

(CYNTHIA *is in the living-room, looking round. A car horn sounds.*)

Oh, there's Maurice.

(MAURICE*'s car pulls into the drive.*)

Come away in.

(ROXANNE *and* PAUL *go into the living-room.* JANE *gets out of* MAURICE*'s car.*)

Hi, Jane!

JANE: (*From outside*) Hello, Monica!

(MONICA *enters the living-room, followed by* JANE.)

MONICA: Oh, this is Jane – Maurice has just been picking her up, from the station.

(MAURICE *enters the hall.*)

CYNTHIA: 'Ere 'e is – 'ello, sweet'eart!

MAURICE: Hiya!

ROXANNE: All right, Maurice?

(*Beaming at her,* MAURICE *closes the front door, and enters the living-room. Beaming back at him,* ROXANNE *offers him the wine.*)

I got you that . . .

MAURICE: (*Taking wine*) You didn't 'ave to do that!

76

ROXANNE: 'T's all right!

MAURICE: (*Quietly*) All right?

ROXANNE: (*Quietly*) Yeah!

> (MAURICE *tickles her momentarily. She giggles.*)
> This is Paul. It's . . . Maurice.

PAUL: All right, mate?

MAURICE: Hiya.

> (*They shake hands.*)

CYNTHIA: Ain't yer got one for me, then?

MAURICE: Yeah – course I 'ave.

CYNTHIA: 'Ello, darlin'! (*She hugs and kisses him.*)

ROXANNE: Don't kill 'im!

CYNTHIA: Cor, you've landed on yer feet 'ere, ain't yer, Maurice?

MAURICE: This is Jane, my lovely assistant.

CYNTHIA: Talked to you on the phone, ain't I, Jane?

JANE: Yeah, that's right.

MONICA: Oh, can I take your coats?

ROXANNE: Yes. (*She takes off her jacket.*)

MAURICE: Right, what d'you want to drink – red, white, rosé, beer?

ROXANNE: Oh, I'll 'ave white, Maurice.

PAUL: Yeah, beer.

> (*He offers the four-pack to* MAURICE, *who takes it.*)

MAURICE: Oh, thanks a lot – cheers.

> (MONICA *takes* CYNTHIA'*s and* ROXANNE'*s coats, and goes out.*)
> Cynth?

CYNTHIA: I'll 'ave white, please, Maurice.

MAURICE: Jane?

JANE: Rosé.

MAURICE: Okey-doke.

> (*He goes out to the hall, where* MONICA *is opening the cupboard.*)

MONICA: Where's the friend, then?

MAURICE: I've no idea.

> (CYNTHIA *joins them.*)

CYNTHIA: 'Ave you got an ashtray, darlin'?

> (MONICA *is hanging up the coats.*)

MONICA: There's one on the coffee-table, Cynthia. I didn't think you would've given up.

CYNTHIA: Oh, one of the few pleasures of life, Monica.

MONICA: (*Of the flowers*) These are very bright.

CYNTHIA: Don't you like 'em?

MONICA: Yeah, I'll just put them in a vase.

> (*She goes into the kitchen.* CYNTHIA *hovers for a moment, then goes back into the living-room, leaving* MAURICE *alone.*)

A short time later, in the living-room. Close-up: little ROXANNE's *portrait on the mantelpiece.*

ROXANNE: What you got that up there for?

MAURICE: We like it.

> (PAUL *sniggers. He and* ROXANNE *are sitting on the sofa, smoking.*)

ROXANNE: (*Smiling*) Oi, don't laugh! (*Of the portrait*) It's stupid.

> (MAURICE *is leaning on the mantelpiece next to the portrait. He is holding a beer.*)

MAURICE: It's one of my early works. You miserable little git.

ROXANNE: He was fuckin' around be'ind the camera.

MAURICE: Oi! Mind your language! Little sod!

> (ROXANNE *giggles. She and* MAURICE *maintain genuine good humour throughout this scene.*)
>
> So how's work, then?

ROXANNE: Oh, it's all right, yeah . . .

MAURICE: Are you still enjoyin' it?

ROXANNE: Yeah, it's all right.

MAURICE: When are you going to college again?

ROXANNE: Shut up about college.

MAURICE: You're going to college, in't yer?

ROXANNE: No, I ain't!

MAURICE: Well, you should do, you've got a good brain.

ROXANNE: But I don't wanna use it, though.

MAURICE: Suit yourself.

ROXANNE: Yeah, I will. Paul's a scaffolder.

MAURICE: Yeah, your mum said. Bet that's hard work, innit?

PAUL: Can be, mate.

MAURICE: Specially in the winter.

PAUL: That's right.

> (MAURICE *chuckles.*)

Meanwhile . . . MONICA *comes out of the kitchen, followed by* JANE *and* CYNTHIA.

MONICA: I wanted to give it a Mediterranean feel.

JANE: Oh, it's a lovely kitchen.

(MONICA *opens a door, to reveal a loo.*)

MONICA: And this is the – oops! (*She goes and lowers the seat, which has been left up.*)

CYNTHIA: Oh, that's a big lavatory!

MONICA: This is the downstairs toilet.

JANE: Oh, that's 'andy, isn't it, 'cos if you're in the garden –

MONICA: (*Adjusting curtains*) Exactly – it's really convenient. And I think the peach tones make it quite tranquil.

JANE: Yeah . . .

MONICA: So you know where it is, if you need it. (*She closes the door, and opens an identical door next to it.*) Now . . . excuse me, Jane . . . this is the garage.

JANE: (*Giggling*) I thought it was the cupboard.

CYNTHIA: Is that a new car?

MONICA: Yes, that's my car.

CYNTHIA: What was the matter with your other one?

MONICA: Nothing. (*She closes the door.*) I'll show you upstairs. (*They all troop upstairs. On the landing is another door.*) We'll start with this. (*She opens it: the airing cupboard.*)

JANE: Oh.

CYNTHIA: There's the tank . . .

MONICA: That's where I keep my towels and bed-linen.

JANE: That's your airing cupboard.

MONICA: Mm. It's not very capacious. (*She closes it, and opens the next door.*) And this is Maurice's bathroom.

JANE: It's green. Matches your tank.

(MONICA *lowers the toilet seat.*)

CYNTHIA: These all new carpets, are they, sweet'eart?

MONICA: Oh, yes! (*She comes out of the bathroom, closes the door, and goes into her bedroom.*) And this is the master bedroom.

CYNTHIA: Cor! It's more like the bridal suite!

JANE: It's beautiful!

MONICA: I've always wanted a four-poster.

CYNTHIA: I can see Maurice thrashing about in there!

MONICA: It is a king-size.

JANE: (*Feeling the nets*) Oh, it's like somethin' out of a fairy tale!

CYNTHIA: I bet this cost a bob or two.

MONICA: (*Adjusting a silk bow*) Well, it certainly wasn't cheap.

CYNTHIA: An 'ere's another lavatory. (*She enters it.*)

MONICA: Oh, that bathroom's mine, the en suite.

CYNTHIA: Oh, you've got one each, 'ave yer? That's nice – ain' it, Jane?

JANE: It's like a hotel.

MONICA: You don't want to be tripping over each other. (*She goes out.*)

JANE: Oh, you got everythin', Monica!

(CYNTHIA *comes out of the loo, and leaves the bedroom.* JANE *follows.*)

Back in the living-room, MAURICE *has sat down.*

MAURICE: So where's this friend, then?

ROXANNE: 'E's 'ere, in' 'e?

MAURICE: No! Your mum's.

ROXANNE: What're you talkin' about?

MAURICE: She rang me at the shop, and asked me if she could bring a friend, from work.

ROXANNE: That's the first I've heard of it.

MAURICE: Is it?

ROXANNE: Yeah.

MAURICE: What, she never mentioned it?

ROXANNE: No!

MAURICE: Peculiar!

ROXANNE: That must be 'oo she's been goin' out with. She's a dark 'orse, in't she?

A little later. MONICA *opens the front door. It is* HORTENSE, *although we can't see her at first, because* MONICA *has only opened the door a little.*

HORTENSE: Hello . . .

MONICA: No, I'm sorry –

HORTENSE: I'm a friend of Cynthia's.

MONICA: Yes, yes – of course . . .

(*She opens the door fully.* HORTENSE *is carrying her coat, and a wrapped present.*)

CYNTHIA: (*From kitchen*) 'Ello, sweet'eart . . .

HORTENSE: Hello!

MONICA: I thought you were –

CYNTHIA: (*Joining them*) Come on in!

>   (HORTENSE *does so.*)

>   That's me mate, 'Ortense.

HORTENSE: Hi!

>   (HORTENSE *and* MONICA *start shaking hands.*)

CYNTHIA: That's me brother's wife.

MONICA: Oh, pleased to meet you. Monica.

HORTENSE: Hello, Monica.

>   (HORTENSE *and* MONICA *are still shaking hands.*)

CYNTHIA: Yeah, well come on out the back, meet me brother.

>   (HORTENSE *and* MONICA *stop shaking hands.*)

HORTENSE: Okay.

>   (*She follows* CYNTHIA. MONICA *closes the front door.*)

MONICA: Can I take your coat for you, em – ?

CYNTHIA/HORTENSE: (*Speaking almost together*) Hortense.

HORTENSE: (*Giving coat*) Thank you.

>   (MONICA *hangs up the coat. As she does so, she observes*
>   CYNTHIA *rubbing* HORTENSE's *back affectionately as they go*
>   *through the kitchen.*)

Outside. CYNTHIA *and* HORTENSE *come through the kitchen door*
on to the patio. MAURICE *is waiting for them.*

CYNTHIA: This is me little brother, Maurice.

HORTENSE: Hello – pleased to meet you, Maurice.

MAURICE: How d'you do?

CYNTHIA: Ain't that little, is 'e? That's Hortense.

MAURICE: Hortense.

HORTENSE: Yeah, that's right.

CYNTHIA: And . . . this is me daughter, Roxanne . . .

HORTENSE: Oh, happy birthday! (*She gives* ROXANNE *the*
>   *present.*) There you go!

CYNTHIA: Oh, you didn't 'ave to do that, sweet'eart!

HORTENSE: 'T's okay!

CYNTHIA: That's Paul, 'er intended.

ROXANNE: 'E ain't me intended! (*She opens the present.*)

HORTENSE: Pleased to meet you.

PAUL: 'Ow d'yer do?

(PAUL *and* HORTENSE *shake hands.*)

CYNTHIA: And this is, um . . .

MONICA: Jane . . .

CYNTHIA: Maurice's assistant.

HORTENSE: Hi!

JANE: Very nice to meet you.

MONICA: Hortense.

HORTENSE: You too.

(CYNTHIA *is examining* HORTENSE*'s present. It is a boxed
bottle of champagne.*)

CYNTHIA: (*To* ROXANNE) Oh, that's nice, innit, sweet'eart? It's
expensive.

MAURICE: What would you like to drink – red, white, rosé?

HORTENSE: White wine, please.

CYNTHIA: You want to put that away – 'ave that tomorrow.

ROXANNE: (*To* HORTENSE) Thanks – that's really nice.

HORTENSE: You're welcome!

ROXANNE: We'll 'ave it later. (*She takes it into the kitchen.*)

CYNTHIA: No, don't waste it!

MONICA: (*Laughing*) I've got some for later, to have with the cake.

JANE: We thought you'd got lost.

HORTENSE: Well, I took a couple of wrong turns.

MONICA: D'you come by minicab, did you?

HORTENSE: No –

CYNTHIA: No, she's got a car.

(ROXANNE *and* MAURICE *return from the kitchen.*)

ROXANNE: It's really nice, that – thanks.

MAURICE: (*Giving* HORTENSE *drink*) There you go.

HORTENSE: Thank you.

MAURICE: Who wants a top-up?

CYNTHIA: I'll 'ave one with you, Maurice.

MONICA: Not for me, thanks!

MAURICE: (*Refilling* JANE*'s glass*) You all right?

JANE: Yeah – so far.

(MONICA *hands round some bowls.*)

MONICA: Would you like some crisps, Hortense?

HORTENSE: No, I'm fine – thanks.

MONICA: A nut? No?

CYNTHIA: I only met Paul for the first time today, 'Ortense.
MONICA: Really?
CYNTHIA: 'E's a scaffolder.
JANE: Are yer?
PAUL: Yeah.
    (MAURICE *has refilled* ROXANNE*'s glass.*)
MAURICE: (*Of the bottle*) Another one bites the dust!
JANE: Hurray!
MONICA: That must be quite dangerous, Paul.
PAUL: Yeah – well, it can be.
    (CYNTHIA *is leaning on a wall.*)
CYNTHIA: (*To* HORTENSE) 'Ere, come and lollop over 'ere.
    (HORTENSE *joins her.*)
JANE: D'you have to go up really high?
PAUL: Sometimes.
    (*Pause.*)
JANE: Just you and the elements, really . . .
MONICA: Ever fallen off? (*She laughs.*) Would you like a crudité,
    Hortense?
HORTENSE: Thank you, no – I think I'll wait till later.
MONICA: Oh . . .

A little while later. CYNTHIA, HORTENSE, ROXANNE, PAUL *and*
JANE *are sitting round the table.* MAURICE *is busy at the barbecue,*
whilst MONICA *bustles about, serving everybody.*
ROXANNE: So you work with my mum, yeah?
HORTENSE: Yeah.
ROXANNE: Not on the machines?
HORTENSE: (*Laughing slightly*) No.
CYNTHIA: You comin' round tomorrow night, Paul?
ROXANNE: Mum!
PAUL: Well, it's –
CYNTHIA: Eh?
ROXANNE: We're goin' out!
    (MONICA *starts collecting everybody's finished corn-cobs.*)
MONICA: (*To* HORTENSE) Just take this . . .
CYNTHIA: Well, you'll come round before'and, won't you, 'ave
    a drink? It's 'er twenty-first.
ROXANNE: It's no big deal!

CYNTHIA: Well, I ain't given you your present yet!

MONICA: Thank you, Jane.

(MAURICE *puts down a dish on the table.*)

MAURICE: Chicken drumsticks . . .

CYNTHIA: D'you want some salad, sweet'eart?

HORTENSE: Yes, please.

CYNTHIA: I'll get you some. (*She goes over to a separate serving table.*)

MONICA: Are you doing something special tomorrow night, you two?

ROXANNE: No, down the pub, as usual.

MONICA: Oh?

JANE: (*To* MAURICE) D'you use fingers?

MAURICE: Use what you like! Use your feet, if you want!
     (JANE *giggles.*)

MONICA: You've a knife and fork there, Jane.

JANE: 'T's a bit late, now.

ROXANNE: What d'you do at the factory, then?

HORTENSE: This really looks lovely, Maurice – thank you!

MAURICE: I hope it dun't kill you!
     (HORTENSE *laughs.*)

MONICA: There's salad there, Cynthia.

ROXANNE: You ain't 'er boss, are you?

HORTENSE: No.

(CYNTHIA *delivers* HORTENSE's *plate.*)

CYNTHIA: 'Ere y'are, sweet'eart.

HORTENSE: Thank you.

CYNTHIA: D'you want some salad, Paul?

PAUL: No, I'm all right, thanks.

CYNTHIA: It's good for you – make you go.

(JANE *giggles.*)

ROXANNE: 'E don't want none.

CYNTHIA: (*To* JANE) What about Jane? Does she want salad?

(JANE *gives* CYNTHIA *her plate.*)

JANE: Yeah – ta very much.

(CYNTHIA *goes back to the serving table.*)

HORTENSE: What do you do, then, Roxanne?

ROXANNE: I work for the council.

JANE: What, down the dole?

ROXANNE: No, I'm a road-sweeper.

HORTENSE: Wow!

JANE: Are you?!

ROXANNE: Yeah.

(MONICA *arrives with a large bowl.*)

MONICA: Who's for a potato?

JANE: She's got my plate!

CYNTHIA: 'Ere you are, sweet'eart!

MONICA: One for you, Hortense?

HORTENSE: Yes – please. Thank you.

ROXANNE: (*To* CYNTHIA) 'Ere, I'll 'ave some o'that, an' all.

CYNTHIA: *Please!*

JANE: Yeah, you do get girl road-sweepers, don't yer?

(MAURICE *returns with more food.*)

MAURICE: Right – burgers and bangers!

ROXANNE: Nice one!

MAURICE: Yeah, that's your one, Roxanne . . . That's the one
with your name on it, the burnt one – all right?

(ROXANNE *laughs.*)

MONICA: Potato for you, Paul?

PAUL: Please. (*He holds out his plate.*)

MONICA: Nice big one.

CYNTHIA: (*Giving* ROXANNE *plate*) 'Ere y'are, darlin'.

MONICA: (*To* ROXANNE) One for you, pet?

ROXANNE: Ta.

CYNTHIA: Shall I do you, Monica?

MONICA: I can see to myself, thanks, Cynthia – why don't you sit down?

CYNTHIA: What about Maurice – 'oo's lookin' after the worker?

MAURICE: Don't worry about me! I've been pickin' – I'll eat later.

HORTENSE: (*Minor accident*) Oops – sorry!

JANE: 'T's all right.

MONICA: Your potato's on your plate there, Cynthia.

CYNTHIA: I think *I'll* 'ave some salad.

MAURICE: Can I have my tongs back, please?

MONICA: Oh, sorry . . . (*She gives them to him.*)

JANE: Got butter?

MONICA: Yes – just a minute!

ROXANNE: I'll have some mustard while you're there, Monica.

MONICA: A-ha? Oh, you like the . . . American, don't you, Roxanne?

ROXANNE: (*Taking it*) Yeah, ta.

(MONICA *gives* JANE *the butter, and picks up her own plate.*)

MONICA: Just get some salad.

JANE: D'you want some butter, Paul?

CYNTHIA: (*To* HORTENSE) You all right, darlin'?

PAUL: (*To* JANE) Great.

HORTENSE: (*To* CYNTHIA) Yeah . . . just waitin' for the butter.

(MAURICE *gives* CYNTHIA *a steak.*)

MAURICE: There you go, Cynth.

CYNTHIA: Oh, Maurice!

ROXANNE: That'll shut you up!

MONICA: Oh? You havin' a steak, are you, Cynthia?

CYNTHIA: Yes – thank you, Monica!

MONICA: (*Sitting*) Well, that'll put hairs on your chest! Like some mustard, or would you prefer the French?

CYNTHIA: (*Ignoring* MONICA) This looks lovely, Maurice!

HORTENSE: (*To* CYNTHIA) Want some of that? (*She refers to the butter.*)

CYNTHIA: Thanks, darlin'.

MAURICE: Right! There you go, mate! Half a cow for you! (*He puts a very large steak on* PAUL's *plate.*)

86

ROXANNE: Fuckin' 'ell! Look at the size of that!!

MONICA: That's ridiculous!

PAUL: Cheers.

CYNTHIA: There's enough there for all of us!

JANE: That'll put some colour in your cheeks, Paul!

MAURICE: Right . . . you're sure no one else wants a steak?

CYNTHIA: Well, ain't you 'avin' one?

MONICA: No, he's not, Cynthia!

MAURICE: Not allowed.

MONICA: Would you like some mustard, Paul?

PAUL: Oh, it's lovely!

CYNTHIA: Can't get rid of it, can yer?

(MAURICE *helps himself to some food, then goes and leans on the adjacent wall.*)

JANE: Oh, it's a real communal thing, eatin'.

MONICA: Yes.

HORTENSE: This is a lovely house.

MONICA: Well, we like it. I'll show you around later, if you want.

HORTENSE: Yeah, thanks – that'd be nice.

JANE: Yeah, it's brilliant!

MONICA: D'you live in a flat, then, Hortense?

HORTENSE: Yeah.

CYNTHIA: Yeah, it's 'er own – she's got a mortgage, an' everything.

MAURICE: Whereabouts are you?

HORTENSE: Kilburn.

MAURICE: That's a bit of a schlepp, innit? The Old Kent Road and back, every day?

HORTENSE: (*Simultaneously*) I just get on the tube.

CYNTHIA: (*Simultaneously*) She drives.

(*Pause.*)

HORTENSE: I drive to the station.

CYNTHIA: You've got a bed-sit, ain't yer, Paul?

PAUL: Yeah, that's right.

MONICA: Ah, that's a shame!

JANE: Wish I 'ad a place o' me own.

HORTENSE: D'you still live at home, then?

JANE: No chance!

87

MAURICE: So, d'you two work on the same machine?

CYNTHIA: No! I'm the only one on slits!

(MAURICE *chuckles*.)

HORTENSE: D'you choose your own workin' hours, then, Roxanne?

ROXANNE: Not bloody likely!

MAURICE: Just bidin' 'er time, till you go to college, aren't you?

ROXANNE: I ain't goin' to college!

CYNTHIA: Hortense went to college.

MONICA: Oh? What did you study?

HORTENSE: Optometry.

JANE: What's that, then?

MAURICE: It's to do with the eye, isn't it?

HORTENSE: 'T's right.

CYNTHIA: Testin'.

MONICA: And you've given that all up now, have you?

HORTENSE: Not exactly . . .

ROXANNE: What're you doin', workin' in a cardboard-box factory, then?

(*Pause*.)

HORTENSE: I'm doing . . . research . . .

MONICA: Oh?

MAURICE: That's interesting. What sort of research?

HORTENSE: Medical.

ROXANNE: What, you lookin' at 'er 'ead?

(*Laughter*.)

CYNTHIA: Take no notice!

HORTENSE: There's nothing wrong with her head.

JANE: D'you go university?

HORTENSE: Yeah.

MAURICE: D'you do a degree?

HORTENSE: Yes, I did.

CYNTHIA: She just looks at our eyes, don't yer?

HORTENSE: (*Laughing*) Yes, I do.

MONICA: What for?

HORTENSE: Well . . . you can tell a lot about people from lookin' at their eyes.

MAURICE: That's true.

MONICA: Can you?

JANE: Windows to your soul.

CYNTHIA: That's a nice way of puttin' it, Jane!

JANE: It's true, though, ain' it?

MAURICE: Right! Who wants a top-up? Hortense?

HORTENSE: No thanks – I'm driving.

CYNTHIA: Yes, please, sweet'eart.

(MAURICE *refills her glass.*)

ROXANNE: (*Holding out her glass*) 'Ere y'are, Maurice.

MAURICE: Oi, greedy-guts.

(HORTENSE *laughs.*)

CYNTHIA: You wanna take a leaf out of 'er book, Paul. (*To* HORTENSE) Lost 'is licence.

(MAURICE *refills* ROXANNE's *glass.*)

ROXANNE: All right, Mum!

JANE: Why, d'you 'ave an accident, Paul?

PAUL: Just 'ad one too many, that's all.

JANE: Oh, shame!

MAURICE: (*Giving* PAUL *beer*) There you go.

MONICA: The demon drink, eh?

PAUL: Ta.

ROXANNE: Is that 'oo you've been goin' out with, then?

(MAURICE *refills* JANE's *glass.*)

CYNTHIA: Yes. She thought I'd been seein' a bloke!

(JANE *and* HORTENSE *laugh.*)

Could've been, I suppose – I can still turn a few 'eads.

ROXANNE: Turn stomachs.

(JANE *lets off a party popper.*)

HORTENSE: Oh!

MONICA: Jane! (*She laughs.*)

JANE: I think it's gone off now – I was just playin'.

ROXANNE: Stupid!

CYNTHIA: 'Ere, d' you want one, 'Ortense?

HORTENSE: (*Quietly*) No.

MONICA: Oh, well – we might as well pop the lot, then!

ROXANNE: No!

(MAURICE *sits down at the table.* JANE *and* MONICA *each let off poppers. Everyone reacts.*)

Later, indoors. MAURICE, *followed by* MONICA, *comes out of the kitchen into the dining-room, which is the back part of the living-room. He carries Roxanne's birthday cake with twenty-one lit candles.*

MAURICE/MONICA: (*Singing*) Happy birthday to you!
    (*The others are all sitting in the front living-room. Heavy rain outside.*)

CYNTHIA/JANE/PAUL: (*Singing*) Happy birthday to you!
    (*A thunderclap outside.* HORTENSE *looks towards the window. She isn't singing.*)

MONICA/CYNTHIA/JANE/PAUL: (*Singing*) Happy birthday, dear Roxanne –

MAURICE: (*Singing, simultaneously*) Happy birthday, dear STINKER!

ROXANNE: Oh, yeah, Maurice – very funny!

CYNTHIA: (*To* HORTENSE) Come on, darlin' – join in!
    (HORTENSE *gets up and joins the others, who are gathering round the cake, which* MAURICE *has put on the table.*)

EVERYONE: Happy birthday to you!!

MAURICE: Hurray!

JANE: Hurray!

MAURICE: Speech!

ROXANNE: Nice one – champagne!
    (MONICA *is passing a bottle to* MAURICE.)

MONICA: Oh, I need my camera – did anybody bring it in?

JANE: I did – it's there, Monica.

ROXANNE: D'you 'ave to, Monica?

MONICA: Of course I have to! (*She gets her camera from a display shelf, and prepares it.*)

ROXANNE: Watch where you point that, Maurice!

MAURICE: All under cover! Okay? And – Whoo!
    (*They turn away, and the cork pops.*)
    Hurray!! (*He pours out the champagne.*)

MONICA: Come on, blow your candles out, Roxanne!
    Everybody else gather round – come on!

CYNTHIA: (*Pulling* HORTENSE) Come on, darlin'.

MAURICE: All right, Cynth – you tuck in there; okay –
    Hortense, in there; right, come round here – Paul; tuck
    yourselves in there . . .

ROXANNE: Hurry up! It's burning me eyebrows off!

MONICA: Right, make a wish! One big blow!

MAURICE: (*Simultaneously*) And –

JANE: (*Simultaneously*) Cheese . . .

(MONICA *snaps her flash camera.*)

MAURICE: Hey!

(ROXANNE *blows several puffs.*)

MONICA: I hope your wish comes true, pet!

MAURICE: (*Gives* ROXANNE *glass*) Roxy.

ROXANNE: Ta.

MAURICE: (*Giving glass*) Right, then, Cynth . . .

CYNTHIA: (*Giving it to* HORTENSE) 'Ere you are, sweet'eart!

ROXANNE: (*Swigging*) Oh, that's nice! Mm . . .

MAURICE: (*Giving glass*) And – Paul . . .

PAUL: Ta, Maurice.

MAURICE: Right . . . (*He gives* CYNTHIA *a glass.*) Cynthia again.

CYNTHIA: Thank you, Maurice. Cor, this is livin', ain' it?

ROXANNE: Mm.

JANE: Yeah!

MONICA: (*To* MAURICE) Thank you!!

MAURICE: (*Pouring own drink*) Okay . . . one for me. Right.

MONICA: (*To* MAURICE) On you go, then.

MAURICE: Oh, yeah . . . okay. Er . . . I would like to propose a
toast . . . to Roxanne, on her twenty-first birthday; now it's
all legal and . . . twice as boring for it. Mind you, it's been
legal since you were eighteen anyway, so I don't know
what I'm talking about.

ROXANNE: (*Laughing*) Yeah!

CYNTHIA: 'Appy birthday, sweet'eart!

MAURICE: Roxanne!

(PAUL *and* HORTENSE *each toast* ROXANNE *inaudibly.*)

MONICA: Happy birthday.

(*Pause.* CYNTHIA *is looking a bit fraught.* MAURICE *takes an
envelope out of his back pocket, and gives it to* ROXANNE.)

MAURICE: There you go.

ROXANNE: What's that?

MAURICE: Book token.

ROXANNE: (*Laughing*) Don't be stupid! (*She opens it. It contains
a birthday card and a wad of paper money.*) Fuckin' 'ell,
Maurice . . . Thanks!

MAURICE: Yeah, well, it's your twenty-first, isn't it?

ROXANNE: Thanks, Monica!

MONICA: Happy birthday, pet! (*She kisses* ROXANNE.) Don't spend it all in the one shop!

MAURICE: Yeah – happy birthday!
  (*He tickles* ROXANNE. *She giggles.*)

CYNTHIA: Wish I'd brought my present wi' me, now.

MAURICE: You can give it to 'er tomorrow, can't you? That's 'er birthday.

CYNTHIA: Yeah, I don't expect I shall see 'er tomorrow! (*To* HORTENSE) Are you gonna sit down, darlin'?
  (MAURICE *watches* CYNTHIA.)

MONICA: Yes, come and sit down, everybody, have some cake, there y'are – Hortense . . .
  (JANE *sits.*)
  Jane . . .

MAURICE: Yeah, get stuck in.
  (MONICA *cuts the cake.*)

ROXANNE: Where am I goin'? 'Ere?

MAURICE: Anywhere you like.
  (CYNTHIA *sits down. She is looking very upset.*)
  I'll get another chair . . .

ROXANNE: Come on the end, Paul . . .

MONICA: (*Giving cake*) Hortense . . .

HORTENSE: (*To* CYNTHIA) Where's the bathroom?

CYNTHIA: It's just through there, sweet'eart.

MAURICE: Yeah, it's the door straight ahead, and the light's on the left.

HORTENSE: Thank you, yeah.

In the loo. HORTENSE *comes in, and shuts the door. She stands for a moment. Then she locks the door. She leans in the corner. She doesn't sit down. She sighs.*

Meanwhile, back at the table, everyone is eating cake.

MAURICE: She's a nice girl.

CYNTHIA: Yeah, she is, Maurice.

MONICA: Seems very pleasant.

ROXANNE: Yeah, she's all right.

92

MONICA: How're you doin', Paul?

PAUL: All right.

MONICA: Has your shirt dried off now? (*She feels his shoulder.*)

CYNTHIA: She takes after her mother.

MAURICE: Does she?

MONICA: D'you know her as well?

MAURICE: Work in the factory, does she?

CYNTHIA: You're lookin' at 'er.

ROXANNE: Eh?

CYNTHIA: She's my daughter.

>   (MAURICE *and* MONICA *look startled.*)

ROXANNE: What's the matter with yer?

CYNTHIA: Maurice . . . it's me daughter.

ROXANNE: Don't be *stupid*! She's 'ad too much to drink.

>   (PAUL *and* JANE *are amused.*)

MONICA: She can't be the one that . . .

>   (MAURICE *looks at her.*)

ROXANNE: What?

>   (MONICA *looks away.*)

CYNTHIA: Hortense, sweet'eart . . . She's yer sister. (*She breaks into tears.*)

ROXANNE: What?

CYNTHIA: (*Fraught*) That's 'er 'alf-sister, Paul.
>   (*Pause.* CYNTHIA *cries. They are all speechless.* HORTENSE *returns. She sits at the table.* CYNTHIA, *in tears:*)
>   You eat your cake, sweet'eart.

HORTENSE: Thanks. What's the matter?

CYNTHIA: I'm all right, darlin'.
>   (HORTENSE *looks round the table.*) I told 'em.
>   (*Pause.* HORTENSE *is nonplussed.*)
>   Tell 'em 'oo you are, sweet'eart.
>   (*Pause.*)

HORTENSE: It wasn't supposed to happen like this.

CYNTHIA: Yeah, well it 'as, ain' it? So you tell 'em – go on.

MAURICE: Is it true?

HORTENSE: Yes, it is.

MAURICE: (*To* CYNTHIA) You never told her, then?

CYNTHIA: (*To* ROXANNE) I'm sorry, darlin' . . .

ROXANNE: Will someone tell me what the fuck's goin' on?

CYNTHIA: SHE'S YOUR SISTER!
  (ROXANNE *looks at* MAURICE.)
ROXANNE: Maurice?
  (MAURICE *is speechless. He lowers his eyes.*)
  Monica?
MONICA: I always said she had a right to know.
  (ROXANNE *registers this for a moment. Then she gets up
  abruptly, and rushes out of the room. Everybody gets up.*
  CYNTHIA *follows* ROXANNE.)
CYNTHIA: Roxanne, sweet'eart, darlin'! Darlin', please!
  (ROXANNE *rushes into the toilet.*)
ROXANNE: Don't you touch me or I will smack you, you slag!
  You fuckin' slag!! Ain't it enough you 'ad to 'ave one
  bastard, you 'ad to 'ave two an' all?!
  (*She pushes* CYNTHIA *out of the toilet.* CYNTHIA *falls, but is
  caught by* MAURICE.)
MAURICE: Stop it!
  (ROXANNE *slams the toilet door.*)
  Roxanne! Roxy!
  (CYNTHIA *comes back into the living-room.*)
CYNTHIA: (*To* HORTENSE) Sit down, darlin' – sit down, Paul.
  (*She sits at the table, and proceeds to eat her birthday cake.*
  HORTENSE *looks at her.*)

94

HORTENSE: Cynthia, I think I should go.

CYNTHIA: (*Grasping* HORTENSE*'s arm*) No, I don't want you to go, darlin' – you sit down! Eat your cake, Jane.

MAURICE: (*In the doorway*) You don't 'alf choose your moments, Cynthia.

CYNTHIA: Well, when's the right moment, Maurice? You tell me that.

(ROXANNE *rushes out of the loo.*)

ROXANNE: Paul, get my coat – we're goin'!

MAURICE: Don't go, Roxy!

ROXANNE: Why didn't you tell me, Maurice?!

MAURICE: I thought you knew.

ROXANNE: You used to tell me everything!

MAURICE: I'm sorry.

ROXANNE: Well, you've fuckin'-well let me down!

MAURICE: Oh, don't say that!

ROXANNE: (*To* HORTENSE) As for you . . . well, thanks for the present! You've ruined my party, and I 'ope you're 'appy! (*She turns round and rushes out.* MAURICE *follows her.*)

MAURICE: Roxy! Roxanne!

(*The front door opens, and* ROXANNE *bursts out, putting her coat on, and followed by* PAUL *and* MAURICE. MONICA *stays in the hall.* ROXANNE *and* PAUL *rush off.* MAURICE *stops outside the house, and lets them go. For a moment, he stands, helpless, hands on hips. Then he walks slowly back to the door. Suddenly, he quickens his pace, grabs his keys from the hall table, rushes out, and, slamming the door behind him, he runs off in* ROXANNE*'s and* PAUL*'s direction.*)

Back inside.

CYNTHIA: (*To* HORTENSE) She don't mean it, darlin'. She's just a little bit upset.

Outside, the rain has stopped, the ground is wet, and the sun is out. At the end of his street, MAURICE *slows down, and looks across the road.* ROXANNE *and* PAUL *are sitting at a bus stop.* MAURICE *goes over.*

MAURICE: Where are you going?

ROXANNE: I don't know.

MAURICE: It's all been a bit of a shock, ennit? Eh?

ROXANNE: Look, I don't get it – did you know about 'er?

MAURICE: Well, I always . . . thought she'd 'ad a boy . . .

ROXANNE: She's a slag.

MAURICE: No, she's not.

ROXANNE: Yes, she fuckin' is.

MAURICE: She loves yer. We all love yer. You comin' back?

ROXANNE: No.

MAURICE: You got to.

ROXANNE: Why should I?

MAURICE: You gotta face up to it!

ROXANNE: Face up to *what*?!

(MAURICE *looks helplessly down the street.*)

In the dining-room. MONICA *picks up* ROXANNE*'s birthday card and money from the table.*

MONICA: She's left her card. Oh, well! I'll post it on to her.

CYNTHIA: I'll take it.

(CYNTHIA *starts clearing the plates.* HORTENSE *and* JANE *are still where they were,* HORTENSE *standing and* JANE *sitting.*)

MONICA: The state she's in, you'll be lucky if you ever see her again.

CYNTHIA: Oh, you'd like that, wouldn't you, sweet'eart?

MONICA: Would I?

CYNTHIA: You've been workin' at it for eighteen years, ain't you, Monica? You turned my father against me, you turned my Maurice against me, and you turned my daughter against me – you'll be 'avin' a go at 'er next, I expect! (*Indicating* HORTENSE.)

MONICA: I'm sorry about this, Hortense – Have you finished there, Jane? (*She takes* JANE*'s plate, and goes towards the door. To* HORTENSE.) Why don't you sit down?

CYNTHIA: You got a short memory, ain't yer?

MONICA: (*Stopping*) What are you talkin' about now?

CYNTHIA: You wouldn't 'ave none of this if I 'adn't given Maurice the money to start with.

MONICA: That money wasn't yours to give – that was your father's insurance money –

CYNTHIA: That money was for me and Roxanne!

MONICA: And Maurice!

CYNTHIA: 'E didn't want none of it till 'e come 'ome and talked to you!

MONICA: He was entitled to it!

CYNTHIA: I was goin' out cleanin' at five o'clock in the mornin', comin' 'ome, takin' 'er to school, an' then goin' out again to do a full day's work.

MONICA: And didn't we know it?!

CYNTHIA: You've done nothin' but spend 'is money since the day you clapped eyes on 'im.

MONICA: Well, what are you supposed to do with money, but spend it? At least we've made something of ourselves!

CYNTHIA: Oh, 'aven't you just?! You want to try bringin' up a kid on your own!

(*Upset,* MONICA *goes out to the kitchen.* CYNTHIA *sobs, watched by* HORTENSE.)

At the bus stop. MAURICE *is now sitting with* ROXANNE *and* PAUL.

MAURICE: She can't 'elp it – she's never 'ad enough love. And you've never got on.

ROXANNE: That ain't my fault.

MAURICE: I know. I know. But she needs yer. Come on . . .

ROXANNE: I don't want to.

MAURICE: What do you think, Paul?

PAUL: I think 'e's right, darlin'.

ROXANNE: Do yer?

PAUL: Yeah.

ROXANNE: Well, I ain't sayin' nothin'!

(*They all start to get up.*)

MAURICE: You won't have to. You just have to listen. Come on.

(*And off they march, single file,* MAURICE *first,* PAUL *last.*)

Back in the living-room. ROXANNE *is listening . . .*

CYNTHIA: I'm sorry, Roxanne. It just came out, darlin'. I didn't mean to spoil your party.

(*She tries to hug* ROXANNE, *who resists violently.*)

ROXANNE: Tell 'er, Maurice!

MAURICE: Now leave 'er alone, Cynth! Just tell 'er the truth.

(CYNTHIA *obeys.*)

CYNTHIA: Darlin' . . . I got pregnant when I was fifteen . . . And your grandad sent me away to this place – didn't 'e, Maurice?

(MAURICE *nods.*)

I didn't know she was gonna come lookin' for me, did I? But I gotta tell you the truth, darlin' – I'm glad she did. It ain' 'er fault, sweet'eart, she didn't even wanna come – she didn't wanna 'urt yer no more 'n I did. Oh, you tell 'er, sweet'eart.

(HORTENSE *is standing with* MONICA. JANE *is still sitting at the table.*)

HORTENSE: It's true. She didn't wanna upset you. I'm sorry.
(*She sits down.*)

MAURICE: (*To* ROXANNE) All right?
(*Pause.*)

CYNTHIA: She said you weren't never gonna come back.

MAURICE: Who did?

MONICA: I never said any such thing – she's twisting everything, as usual.

CYNTHIA: Yes, you did, Monica! Well, you was wrong, wa'n't yer, 'cos she 'as come back, ain't yer, sweet'eart?
(*She tries to cuddle* ROXANNE, *who again pushes her off.*)

MONICA: I always thought you should've known, Roxanne.

MAURICE: You should've told her, Cynth.

CYNTHIA: Of course I should've told 'er, Maurice. But I didn't think there was ever gonna be no need to. You seem to 'ave told all and sundry.

MONICA: Meaning me, I suppose! And why shouldn't he? I am his wife, after all!

CYNTHIA: Then why don't you be'ave like 'is wife?

MONICA: What?

CYNTHIA: Why don't you give 'im no kids?

MAURICE: Be quiet, Cynthia.

MONICA: That's between Maurice and me.

CYNTHIA: You're so selfish, Monica – you might not 'ave wanted 'em, but 'e did!

ROXANNE: Shut up, Mum!

MAURICE: You don't know what you're talkin' about!

CYNTHIA: Don't I?

MAURICE: There are things you know nothing about.

MONICA: Maurice!

CYNTHIA: Like what?
(*Pause.*)

MAURICE: Tell 'er.
(*Pause.*)

CYNTHIA: Tell me what?

99

(*Pause.*)

MAURICE: Why can't you tell 'er? (*Pause.*) She can't have kids.
Simple as that. She's physically incapable of having
children. We've had every test known to medical science.
She's been pushed around, prodded, poked, had
operations – we've had fifteen years of it, and she can't
have a baby. (*To* MONICA) I love you to bits . . . but it's
almost destroyed our relationship . . . you know it has.

There. I've said it. So where's the bolt o' lightning?
(*Pause.*) Secrets and lies! We're all in pain. Why can't we
share our pain? I've spent my entire life trying to make
people 'appy, and the three people I love the most in the
world 'ate each other's guts, I'm in the middle AND I
CAN'T TAKE IT ANY MORE!!!

(*Long pause. Everybody is shaken.* MONICA *weeps, fraught.
Then* MAURICE *goes over to* HORTENSE.)

I'm sorry, Hortense. But you are a very brave person.

HORTENSE: A very stupid person.

MAURICE: No, you're not. You wanted to find the truth, and
you were prepared to suffer the consequences. And I
admire you for that. I mean it.

(*He sits beside her at the table.* ROXANNE *looks at them.* PAUL
looks at ROXANNE. CYNTHIA *looks at* MONICA. MONICA
weeps. CYNTHIA *gets up and goes over to* MONICA. *She takes
her in her arms.* MONICA *sobs.* MAURICE *watches them.*)

MONICA: You're so lucky, Cynthia.

(PAUL *half puts his arm round Roxanne, who is more
concerned with* CYNTHIA *and* MONICA.)

MAURICE: Have you really been working in the factory?

HORTENSE: No.

MAURICE: What d'you do, then?

HORTENSE: I'm an optometrist.

(MAURICE *chuckles.*)

MAURICE: Welcome to the family.

JANE: (*In tears*) Oh . . . Maurice . . . I wish I'd had a dad like
you. You're lovely.

(MAURICE *leans across the table, and takes her hand.*
CYNTHIA *is still nursing* MONICA *in her arms.*)

CYNTHIA: (*To* ROXANNE) 'Is name's Bingham . . . yer father

. . . he's from America. I met 'im on 'oliday. Benidorm.
'E's a medical student. And one morning I come down,
and 'e wasn't there no more . . . But 'e was a nice man. 'E
was.
(*Tears begin to well in* ROXANNE*'s eyes.*)
HORTENSE: Was my father a nice man?
CYNTHIA: Oh, don't break my heart, darlin'!
(*After a few moments, she breaks down, sobbing uncontrollably.*
MONICA *puts her arm round her.* ROXANNE *starts to cry.*
MAURICE *touches* HORTENSE.)
HORTENSE: I'm all right. (*She looks at* CYNTHIA *and*
MONICA. *Then she gets up and joins them, hugging* CYNTHIA.)
CYNTHIA: (*Through her crying*) Please, Roxanne . . . sweet'eart
. . . please!!
(ROXANNE *does not move, but she cries.*)

That night. MAURICE *and* MONICA *are in bed.*
MAURICE: I'm frightened.
MONICA: Why?
MAURICE: You don't love me any more. Not like you used to.
(MONICA *turns towards him.*)
MONICA: Maurice . . . (*She strokes his face.*) You don't know
how much I love you.
MAURICE: Do you?
(*She kisses him.*)
We've got each other, haven't we?
(*They rub noses, and hold each other lovingly.*)

A bright, sunny day. HORTENSE*'s car is parked outside* CYNTHIA
and ROXANNE*'s house.*

In the back garden, ROXANNE *and* HORTENSE *are peering into the
dilapidated remains of the greenhouse, which is full of junk.*
ROXANNE: Bet you've never seen so much shit, 'ave yer?
HORTENSE: (*Laughing*) You wanna see my mum's 'ouse.
ROXANNE: D'you miss 'er?
HORTENSE: Yeah.
ROXANNE: Did you get on with er?
HORTENSE: She used to drive me mad! (*She laughs.*)

ROXANNE: That's what they're there for, though, ain't it?
HORTENSE: Yeah . . .
　　　(*Amongst the junk, an old baby's high-chair.*)
ROXANNE: That's me old chair there.
HORTENSE: Ah! I always wanted a little sister. No, it's just that
　　　my brothers were so much older than me, so I ended up
　　　playin' on my own most of the time.
ROXANNE: Oh, I know what you mean.
　　　(*Pause.* HORTENSE *laughs.*)
　　　What're you laughin' at?
HORTENSE: D'you feel like we're sisters?
ROXANNE: I dunno . . . Do you?
　　　(HORTENSE *makes a 'dunno' noise.*)
　　　'S a bit weird.
HORTENSE: Yeah . . .
ROXANNE: I don't mind it, though.
HORTENSE: No. Nor do – nor do I.
ROXANNE: I don't even know you yet, do I?
　　　(HORTENSE *laughs.*)
　　　D'you wanna go out one night?
HORTENSE: Yeah . . . Yeah! You can take me to one o' your
　　　pubs.
ROXANNE: Yeah, all right.

HORTENSE: How would you introduce me? As your half-sister?

ROXANNE: Yeah.

HORTENSE: No, man. Too much explainin' to do.

ROXANNE: That's what I'd say, though.

HORTENSE: Would you?

ROXANNE: Yeah!

HORTENSE: (*After a moment*) Yeah. Best to tell the truth, innit?

ROXANNE: Yeah, it is.

HORTENSE: That way, nobody gets 'urt.

(*We cut to a high shot, the camera looking down on the garden from above.* CYNTHIA *comes out of the house with a laden tray.*

CYNTHIA: 'Ere y'are, sweet'eart – tea's up! Go on, darlin'!
Wanna biscuit?

HORTENSE: No, I'm all right – thank you . . .

CYNTHIA: Right, sit yerself down.

(ROXANNE *sits on a chair,* HORTENSE *on a stool.*)

HORTENSE: You all right with that?

CYNTHIA: Yeah! (*She sits on her old sunbed, puts her feet up, and places the tray on the ground.*) That's it. Cor . . . 'Oo'd 'ave thought it, eh? Look at you two, sitting there – like a couple o' garden gnomes! (*She laughs.*) Cor . . . Oh, this is the life, ain' it?

HORTENSE/ROXANNE: Yeah.

And the three of them enjoy the afternoon together.